Kirk Munroe

Prince Dusty

a story of the oil regions

Kirk Munroe

Prince Dusty
a story of the oil regions

ISBN/EAN: 9783744741521

Printed in Europe, USA, Canada, Australia, Japan

Cover: Foto ©ninafisch / pixelio.de

More available books at **www.hansebooks.com**

RAIL AND WATER SERIES

PRINCE DUSTY

A STORY OF THE OIL REGIONS

BY

KIRK MUNROE

AUTHOR OF "UNDER ORDERS," "THE FLAMINGO FEATHER,"
"DERRICK STERLING," "DORYMATES,"
"CAMPMATES," etc., etc.

ILLUSTRATED

G. P. PUTNAM'S SONS
NEW YORK   LONDON
27 WEST TWENTY-THIRD ST.   27 KING WILLIAM ST., STRAND
The Knickerbocker Press
1891

CONTENTS.

CHAPTER
I.—A Prince and Princess Go in Search of Adventures 1
II.—A Present from a Fairy God-Mother . 8
III.—Brace Barlow the "Moonlighter" . 17
IV.—A Torpedo Man's Peril 25
V.—Arthur and His Cousins . . 33
VI.—A Gallant Rescue and Its Reward . 40
VII.—Uncle Phin's Plan 49
VIII.—Awakened at Midnight 58
IX.—A Hurried Flight 66
X.—On Board the Ark 74
XI.—Uncle Phin's Danger 82
XII.—A Torrent of Flame 90
XIII.—How the Ark was Saved . . 98
XIV.—A Camp of Tramps 107
XV.—Arthur's Fight to Save Rusty . . 115
XVI.—The Meaning of Some Queer Signs . 123
XVII.—Pleasant Driftings 130
XVIII.—The Ark is Stolen . . . 139

CHAPTER	PAGE
XIX.—Penniless Wanderers in a Strange City	148
XX.—A Railroad Experience	154
XXI.—Carried Off in a Freight Car	164
XXII.—Saving the Keystone Express	172
XXIII.—Crossing the Alleghanies	182
XXIV.—A Brave Struggle with Poverty	189
XXV.—Finding a Home	199
XXVI.—Colonel Dale of Dalecourt	207
XXVII.—A "Genuine Chump"	216
XXVIII.—A Few Facts Concerning Petroleum	224
XXIX.—Locating an Oil Well	234
XXX.—The Dale-Dustin Mystery	243
XXXI.—A Bitter Disappointment	250
XXXII.—Shooting a "Duster"	259
XXXIII.—Saved by the Sign of the Tramp	266
XXXIV.—An Oil Scout Outwitted	274
XXXV.—Developing an Oil Region	283
XXXVI.—Arthur Remembers His Friends	290

ILLUSTRATIONS.

	PAGE
ONE OF THE GREAT OIL TANKS HAD BEEN STRUCK BY LIGHTNING, AND NOW A RAGING, ROARING MASS OF FLAME SHOT UP.	*Frontispiece*
PRINCE DUSTY AND CYNTHIA SET OUT ON THEIR ADVENTURES	4
PRINCE DUSTY AND HIS FAIRY GODMOTHER	8
A HURRIED FLIGHT BY MOONLIGHT	70
STANDING STEADILY IN THE MIDDLE OF THE TRACK HE SWUNG HIS DANGER SIGNAL TO AND FRO	180
THE FAIRY GODMOTHER FINDS PRINCE DUSTY	198
WITH A MIGHTY ROAR LIKE THAT OF THUNDER, A DENSE VOLUME OF GAS BURST FORTH	264
"YES, THAT'S SANDY'S MARK," SAID ONE OF THEM, "THERE'S NO GOING BACK ON THAT"	272

PRINCE DUSTY

A STORY OF THE OIL REGIONS.

CHAPTER I.

A PRINCE AND PRINCESS GO IN SEARCH OF ADVENTURES.

TWELVE-YEAR-OLD Arthur Dale Dustin did not look the least bit like a Prince, sitting perched on the topmost rail of the zig-zag fence that bright September afternoon. As he dangled his bare brown legs idly, he wistfully watched his cousins at the play in which they would not allow him to join. He loved to play as dearly as any other boy; but somehow or other he was always left out of their games by the boisterous crew of little Dustins whom he called cousins. He tried his best to like what they liked, and to be one with them; but something always seemed to happen to prevent.

Once when they all went to see the well that his uncle, John Dustin, was drilling, deep down into the ground, with the hope of striking petroleum, they found the men away, and, for a few minutes, had the place to themselves. Thereupon Cousin Dick, who was two years older than Arthur, climbed up the derrick, and, watching his chance, sprang on the end of the great walking beam, that was working slowly up and down with ponderous strokes. Here he rode on the back of his mighty wooden steed for a few seconds, while the other children shouted and clapped their hands with admiration.

Then Dick came down and dared Arthur to perform the same feat; but the boy held back. He was not afraid, not a bit of it; and even if he had been he would gladly have done anything Dick dared do, merely to win his good-will and that of the others. But his Uncle John had forbidden them even to go near the derrick or the engine unless he was there to look after them. The others seemed to have forgotten this; but Arthur remembered it, and so refused to ride on the walking beam because it would be an act of disobedience. Then Cousin Dick sneered at him, and called him a "'Fraid-cat," and all the others, except tender-hearted, freckle-faced little Cynthia, took up the cry and shouted, "'Fraid-cat! 'Fraid-cat!" as they crowded around him and pushed him into the derrick.

Just then Uncle John returned and the others ran away, leaving poor Arthur, looking very confused and red in the face, standing in the middle of the derrick floor. Then, when his uncle in a stern voice asked him what he was doing in that place which he had been strictly forbidden to enter, Arthur hung his head and would not say anything; for he was too brave a lad to be a "tell-tale," and too honest to tell a lie. So his Uncle John said that he was a naughty boy who had led the other children into mischief, and that he might go right home and get into bed, and stay there for the rest of the day as a punishment.

Poor Arthur obeyed; and, as he walked slowly toward the only place in the world he could call his home, great tears rolled down his cheeks. When the other children, who were hiding in the bushes, saw them they called out, "Cry-baby! Cry-baby!"

Only little Cynthia ran out and put her arm about his neck and said she was sorry; but Dick pulled her roughly away.

Another time when Cynthia asked Arthur to build a house for her dolls, under the roots of a great tree that had blown down just on the edge of the woods back of the house, he, being an obliging little soul, consented at once to do so. Under the huge mass of roots and earth they played happily enough at making believe it was a cave, and Cynthia was radiant with delight over the beautiful time they were having. For a little while Arthur experienced the novel feeling of being perfectly happy. Then, all of a sudden, a shower of earth and gravel came rattling down on them from above, and with it came a mocking chorus of "Girl-boy! Girl-boy! Look at the girl-boy playing with dolls!" and little Cynthia began to cry over the ruin of her beautiful baby-house.

Upon this, with a quick blaze of indignation, Arthur picked up a bit of stick and flung it with all his strength at the tormentors who had brought tears to his little cousin's eyes. It was aimed at nobody in particular; but it happened to strike Dick on the cheek and make a slight cut, from which the

PRINCE DUSTY AND CYNTHIA SET OUT ON THEIR ADVENTURES. (*Page* 5.)

blood flowed. Thereupon the big boy ran crying home to his mother, and told her that Arthur had struck him with a stick, in proof of which story he showed his bloody face. Then Mrs. Dustin, who always acted upon the impulse of the moment, took down the apple switch from over the mantel-piece and gave her nephew a whipping, which she said would be a lesson to him. Poor little Cynthia tried to explain how it had all happened; but her mother had no time to listen, and only told her and the other children to come away from the bad boy, and not go near him again that day.

Some days after this, when all the others had gone on a fishing expedition, upon which they had refused to let Arthur and Cynthia accompany them, the boy proposed a beautiful plan to his little cousin. He remembered the fairy tales his own dear mother used to read to him, and now he said:

"Let us make believe we are a Prince and Princess, Cynthia, and go out into the world in search of adventures."

Cynthia had not the remotest idea of what was meant by "adventures"; but she was willing to agree to anything that Arthur might propose.

So the two children set forth, and nobody noticed them as they went out of the front gate and walked, hand in hand, down the dusty road.

They had not gone far before they discovered a poor little robin just learning to fly, that had fallen into a ditch by the roadside, where in a few moments more he would have been drowned. Of course they rescued him, and, while the old mother and father birds flew about them uttering cries of distress and begging them not to hurt their baby, Cynthia dried his wings and carefully wiped the mud from his downy feathers with her pinafore. Then Arthur climbed over a fence and gently placed the little trembling thing down in the soft grass on the other side.

Next they found a yellow butterfly, whose pretty wings were all tangled in a spider's web. Of course they set him free, and had the pleasure of seeing him flutter joyously away. Arthur said these were beautiful adventures, and both the children looked eagerly forward to finding some more; but they walked nearly a mile, and were becoming very hot and tired, before they met with another.

All of a sudden, as they were passing a cottage by

the roadside, they were startled by a deep, loud bark, and turning they saw a big Newfoundland dog bound over the front fence, and come dashing directly toward them. Now, while Arthur was very fond of dogs that he was acquainted with, he was also very much afraid of strange dogs, especially big ones; and his first impulse upon this occasion was to run away. Then he remembered that he was a Prince, and that princes were always brave. So he told Cynthia to run as fast as she could, and hide in the bushes. As she did this the brave little fellow turned a bold front, though he was trembling in every limb, toward the enemy. The next instant the big dog sprang upon him, threw him down, rolled him in the dust, and then stood over him wagging a bushy tail, and barking with delight at what he had done.

CHAPTER II.

A PRESENT FROM A FAIRY GOD-MOTHER.

ARTHUR, who thought he was certainly to be killed, shut his eyes, and for nearly a minute lay perfectly still. He opened them on hearing a trampling of hoofs, a jingling of harness, and a loud "Whoa." Then, no longer seeing the dog, he quickly scrambled to his feet. He was right under the noses of a pair of splendid horses, and behind them was a fine carriage, from which a beautiful lady was just stepping.

"Why, little boy," she said, as she took Arthur's hand and led him away from in front of the horses, "don't you know that you came very near being run over? and that it is dangerous to be playing out here in the middle of the road? Now run into the house, and ask your mother to brush your clothes, and don't ever do so again."

PRINCE DUSTY AND HIS FAIRY GODMOTHER. (*Page* 8.)

"But I don't live here," said Arthur, lifting his dust-covered little face to the gracious one bent down to him. "I live a long way off, and I'm a Prince, and Cynthia is a Princess, and we were looking for adventures, when a big dog knocked me down; but he did n't hurt Cynthia, because I defended her, the same as princes do in the stories my own mamma used to read to me."

"So you are a Prince, are you?" laughed the lady; "then you must be 'Prince Dusty.' Well, if you will get into my carriage, and show me the way, I will take you home to your castle. But where is your Princess? What did you say her name was?"

"It is Cynthia," replied Arthur, "and there she comes now."

As he spoke, poor, terrified little Cynthia came timidly out from the bushes where she had been hiding, and crying with fright, for the last three minutes.

Then the beautiful lady took them both into her carriage, and ordered the coachman to drive on, while she soothed and comforted the children, and wiped Arthur's dusty face with her own embroidered handkerchief.

She looked curiously at him when he told her that his name was Arthur Dale Dustin, that his dearest mamma and papa were dead, and that he used to live in New York, but that now he lived with Cynthia's father and mother, who were his Uncle John and Aunt Nancy. She asked him several questions about himself; but always seemed to forget his name and only called him "Prince Dusty."

When they reached the Dustin house she kissed both the children good-bye, and gave Arthur a beautiful copy of Hans Christian Andersen's "Fairy Tales," that she had in the carriage with her. On the fly-leaf she wrote, with a tiny gold pencil that hung from her watch-chain: "To Prince Dusty from his Fairy God-mother." Then she said she must hurry on, and drove away, leaving the children standing by the roadside and staring after the carriage so long as the faintest cloud of dust from its wheels was visible.

As they turned slowly into the front gate, and walked toward the house, Arthur drew a long breath and said: "Cynthia, that is the very most beautiful adventure I ever heard of. It's beautifuller even than the stories my own mamma used to tell, and I've got this lovely book to show that it is all true."

Poor Arthur was not allowed to enjoy the possession of his book very long, for his Aunt Nancy, who had been alarmed at the children's disappearance, and now gave them only bread and water for their dinner, took it from him, and laid it on a high shelf, saying that it was altogether too handsome a book for a little boy to have.

Arthur begged, and pleaded with tears in his eyes, that he might be allowed to keep his book, claiming justly that it was his very own, and had been given to him to do as he pleased with; but all to no purpose. His Aunt Nancy only said that she would give it to him when the proper time came; and then, adding that she was too busy now to be bothered with him, she bade him get out of the house, and not let her see him again before sundown.

So the sensitive little chap walked slowly away, trying in vain to choke back the indignant sobs that would persist in making themselves heard, and feeling very bitterly the injustice of his Aunt Nancy's action. He longed for sympathy in this time of trial, and for some friendly ear into which he might pour his griefs. Even Cynthia's company was denied him, for she was seated in the kitchen under her mother's watchful eye, taking slow, awkward stitches in the patchwork, a square of which was her allotted task for each day.

"I'll find Uncle Phin," said Arthur to himself, "and tell him all about it, and perhaps he will somehow find a way to get my book again, and then I'll ask him to take me away from here, to some place where I can keep it always."

Somewhat cheered by having a definite purpose in view, the forlorn little fellow started across the fields toward a distant wood lot, in which he knew his sympathizing old friend and adviser was at work.

Uncle Phin was a white-headed, simple-hearted, old negro, who, some years before, had been a slave belonging to Colonel Arthur Dale, of Dalecourt, Virginia. He had been the constant attendant, in her daily horseback rides, of the Colonel's only daughter, the lovely Virginia Dale, to whom her father had formally presented him, as a birthday gift, when she was fifteen years old.

Three years later the spirited girl, refusing to marry the man whom her father had selected for her, ran away with Richard Dustin, a young Northerner recently graduated from a New England university, who had accepted a professorship in one of the Virginia colleges. This marriage proved so terrible a disappointment to her father that, in his anger, he declared he would never receive a communication from her, nor see her again, and he never did. The young couple, accompanied by the faithful Uncle Phin, went to New York. There their only child, a boy, named Arthur Dale after the grandfather who refused to recognize him, was born, and there they lived in the greatest happiness until the child was nearly eleven years old. Then the beautiful young mother died, leaving Richard Dustin utterly heartbroken. Soon afterward he removed with his idolized boy and Uncle Phin, who had filled the position of nurse and constant protector to Arthur from infancy, to the home of his childhood, a little rocky farm in Northwestern Pennsylvania.

He had but one relative in the world, a brother, who lived near one of the mushroom-like towns that sprang up during the early days of petroleum. When, a year after the death of his wife, Richard Dustin was also laid in the grave, it was in the family of this brother, John Dustin, that Arthur and Uncle Phin found a home.

Richard Dustin left no property save the rocky farm that was too poor even to support a mortgage. As his brother John had a large family, the new burdens now thrust upon him were not very warmly welcomed. In fact Mrs. Dustin strongly urged her husband not to receive them. She was Arthur's Aunt Nancy, a hard, unsympathetic, overworked woman, who grudged every morsel of food that the new-comers ate, and seemed to consider that everything given to Arthur was just so much stolen from her own children.

Uncle Phin, it is true, worked faithfully to do what he could toward earning the bread eaten by himself and his "lil Marse," as he persisted in calling Arthur, but he was old and feeble, and the best that he could do did not amount to much. The scanty, but neat, city-made wardrobe that Arthur brought with him to his new home, had not been replenished by a single garment, and now the boy's clothes were shabby and outgrown to such a degree, that his mother's heart would have ached could she have seen him.

Although he was a thoughtful, imaginative child, he was remarkably strong and active for his age. He had learned to read and write at his mother's knee, and his father had, during the last year of his life, found his only pleasure in planning and directing the boy's education. Arthur was therefore as far in advance of his cousins in this respect as he was in refinement and ideas of honor. He was so very different from them that, though he tried hard to love them and make them love him, they, with the exception of little Cynthia, to whom he was an ideal of perfection, united in cordially disliking him.

This dislike was clearly shown, and resulted in many a heartache and many an unjust punishment to the lonely orphan boy. Many a night he slipped from his little cot bed in the back shed, and creeping to where Uncle Phin slept on a hay-mow in the barn, poured his troubles with bitter tears into the sympathetic ears of the old negro.

Then the faithful soul would open wide his arms, and nestling the fair head of his "lil Marse" against his broad bosom, would soothe and comfort him with gentle croonings and quaint quavering plantation melodies. His singing was always accompanied by a slow rocking motion of the body, and finally the blue, tear-swollen eyes would close, and the boy would drop into a sleep full of beautiful dreams, in which he always saw his own dear father and mother. Then Uncle Phin's frosted head would droop lower and lower, until he too was asleep and dreaming of his long ago cabin home under the magnolia trees of old Virginia. Thus these two would comfort each other until morning.

Now, choking with a sense of injustice and wrong at the hands of his Aunt Nancy, little Prince Dusty fled across the fields in search of this friend. He was filled with the determination to beg Uncle Phin to take him away from that hated place, to some other where they might live happily together for always and always.

CHAPTER III.

BRACE BARLOW THE MOONLIGHTER.

BESIDES Uncle Phin and Cynthia, Arthur had one other friend whom he seldom saw now, but whom he was always glad to meet. This was Brace Barlow, a stalwart, good-natured, young fellow, about twenty-five years old, who seemed so big and strong to the little boy, that the latter called him his "dear giant." He worked for Arthur's uncle when the boy first came to live with the Dustins, and had immediately taken a great fancy to the gentle little fellow. He taught Arthur to ride horseback, to drive a team, and to swim, and was always ready to tell him stories of adventures in the oil region. Besides these things, he took pains patiently to explain where the oil came from, and how wells were drilled, deep down into the earth to its hiding-places.

Some months before the time with which this story opens, Brace Barlow left Mr. Dustin's employ, and, much to Arthur's dismay, became a "moonlighter."

Now to understand what a "moonlighter" is, one must know at least as much as Arthur did about oil wells. They are holes about the size of an ordinary stove-pipe, bored, by means of immensely heavy iron drills, hundreds and sometimes thousands of feet into the earth, until they reach the layer of porous sandstone that holds the oil, just as a sponge holds water.

With the oil in this sandstone are vast quantities of gas, that exert an enormous pressure upon it; and the moment an opening is made to where it is, this gas forces the oil to the surface, often driving it forth in great spurts and fountain-like jets. Such a well is called a "gusher," and from it the oil flows for days, weeks, and sometimes for years. After a while, however, the supply of oil or gas, or both, becomes exhausted, so that the stream no longer rises above the mouth of the well. Then a pump is used, and by means of it the oil is pumped up, just as water is from an ordinary well. But the supply of oil always decreases, until, by and by, the pump no longer brings it up in paying quantities.

For some years after the discovery of oil, these exhausted wells were abandoned, and their owners sunk new ones in other places. At length, however, a wise man who had studied the situation very carefully, concluded that if, by any means, the oil-bearing rock could be shattered for a considerable distance around the bottom of these old wells, the flow of oil might be increased, and it might again be produced from them in paying quantities. So he invented a torpedo that could be exploded at any required depth in a well. It was simply a long tin tube, closed at the lower end, and filled with nitro-glycerine. This is one of the most terrible explosives ever discovered; and though it is only ordinary sweet glycerine, such as is used for chapped faces and hands, mixed with nitric acid, it is ten times more powerful than gunpowder, and explodes upon receiving a very slight shock or blow.

A torpedo of this kind, lowered to the bottom of an oil well, and exploded by means of a sharp-pointed iron weight dropped upon it, shatters a large area of oil-bearing rock, and the oil or gas, comes rushing to the surface as when the well was first opened. This operation is called "shooting a well"; the lowering of a torpedo into position, a thousand feet or more below the surface of the earth, is called "placing a shot," and the men who undertake this dangerous business are called "torpedo men" or "well-shooters."

The person who invented this process of well-shooting, and obtained a patent on it, charged so much for the use of his torpedoes that to shoot a well was an expensive undertaking. Many oil producers thought they could not afford it, or that their exhausted wells were not worth the further expenditure of so much money. Under these circumstances a class of reckless, daring fellows sprang into existence, who made a business of manufacturing torpedoes, and secretly shooting wells without paying the inventor the royalty to which his patent entitled him. Thus they were able to do the work much more cheaply than the regular torpedo men, and a great number of well owners were willing to employ them for the sake of what money they would thus save.

As these men generally worked at night they were called "moonlighters," and many thrilling tales of the desperate risks run by them, are still told in the oil regions. The inventor of the torpedo, who was the only man having a legal right to use it, was of course most anxious to detect and punish these "moonlighters," and for this purpose he employed a number of spies. These spies, or detectives, were generally mounted on fleet horses, and whenever they discovered a "moonlighter" driving along the lonely roads, with his load of nitro-glycerine, they gave chase to him. Then he would whip up his spirited team, and drive away at full speed, reckless of consequences, and only intent upon escaping from his pursuers.

Thus it often happened that people sleeping in the vicinity of those quiet mountain roads were awakened at night by the sound of galloping horses, the rattle of a light wagon, and the shouts of its pursuers. They would hold their breath and wait in anxious suspense until the sounds died away, happy if they did not hear the awful roar of an explosion, that meant instant death to all who were anywhere near that ill-fated wagon.

When it is remembered that such an explosion could be caused by the breaking of a wheel, the upsetting of the wagon, or even its sudden striking against a rock or stump, and that such an accident would result in the instantaneous and complete disappearance of men, horses, wagon, and everything within reach of the awful stuff, it will be understood what terrible risks the "moonlighters" ran in pursuit of their illegal business, and what reckless men they were. As the patent on oil-well torpedoes expired some years ago, and anybody can now use them who chooses to do so, there are no longer any "moonlighters," but at the time of this story they were numerous, and Arthur's friend, Brace Barlow, was one of the most daring of them all.

To have his "dear giant" engage in a pursuit at once so wrong and so dangerous was a great grief to the honest, loving little soul, and at every opportunity he pleaded with Brace to give it up. But the young man would only laugh, saying that he had as much right to shoot wells and risk his life as anybody else, and that it was the easiest way of making money he knew of.

At length, however, about daylight one morning, he came to the Dustin house, bruised, bleeding, and with an awe-stricken look on his usually merry face.

Waking his little friend, he said he had come to tell him that his moonlighting days were over, and that hereafter he was to be an honest well-shooter, in the service of the rightful owner of the torpedo patent.

"Oh, I am so glad!" cried the boy, "only I wish you would work at something else, and never touch the awful glycerine again."

"I can't give it up entirely, little one," replied Brace. "Its very danger makes it exciting, and any other life would seem tame after it."

"Well," said Arthur, "if you must be one, I am glad you are going to be an honest torpedo man. But, 'dear giant,' are you hurt? What makes you look so queer?"

Then Brace told him that about an hour before, he had been driving quietly along, with fifty quarts of nitro-glycerine stowed snugly under his buggy seat, toward a well that he was to shoot at daylight, when the sound of galloping hoofs gave warning that a detective was on his track. He instantly whipped up his horses, and, as they sprang forward, his light buggy was nearly upset by striking some obstacle, and he was thrown to the ground with such force as to be partially stunned. As he lay there the detective dashed past without noticing him, and overtaking the runaway team a minute later probably tried to stop them. They must have swerved to one side, the buggy had undoubtedly been upset, and a terrific explosion instantly followed. When Brace reached the spot no trace of man, horses, or wagon, was to be found, and only a great hole in the ground marked the scene of the catastrophe.

The boy shuddered as he listened to this story, and for days afterward his sunny face was clouded by its memory. Still he found some comfort in reflecting that nothing less than some such terrible lesson would have made an honest torpedo man of his dear "moonlighter," with whom, from that time forward, his friendship became stronger than ever.

CHAPTER IV.

A TORPEDO MAN'S PERIL.

ON the day that Arthur played at being a Prince, and was on his way to unfold the sad result of that experience to Uncle Phin, he met Brace Barlow driving out of an old wood road that led to his nitro-glycerine magazine, hidden in the loneliest depths of the forest.

At sight of his little friend, Brace reined in his horses and stopped for a moment's chat with him.

In spite of the young man's warning that he had a load of the "stuff" under the seat, Arthur ran forward and clambered up into the wagon beside him.

"Oh, I am so glad to see you, 'dear giant'!" he began impulsively, "because——" Here he paused.

He had been about to pour into this friend's ear all his troubles, and make a complaint against his

Aunt Nancy; but it suddenly occurred to him that by so doing he would be only acting the part of a tale-bearer, which his father had taught him most heartily to despise. Telling things to Uncle Phin was different. He was quite certain that Brace could not help him in his present trouble, and so, when the latter asked with a smile, "Because what, little one?" he answered:

"Because I love you, and I am always glad to see the people I love. Are you going to shoot a well? Can't I go with you? Aunt Nancy says I am to stay out of her sight until sunset, and the boys have gone fishing, and Cynthia's doing her patchwork, and I have n't a single thing to do. Please let me go."

"Well, I don't know," replied Brace Barlow, reflectively. "I don't suppose there is really any danger; still——"

"Danger!" exclaimed Prince Dusty, scornfully. "Do you suppose I am any more afraid of danger than you are, even if you are a great, big man and I am only a little boy? Well, I'm not. Your old glycerine can't be any worse than lightning, and I'm not a bit afraid of that. Besides, if

I am always going to live in this oil region, I ought to learn all about its dangers, so that I'll know enough to keep away from them. Perhaps when I have grown to be a giant, like you, I will want to be a well-shooter too, and how can I if I have n't learned how?"

This array of argument was too much for Brace to answer, and so, saying, "Well, I suppose I'll have to take you with me just this once," he chirruped to his horses, and, driving much more slowly and carefully than usual, turned into the road that led to the well he was engaged to shoot.

They reached the place without incident, and Arthur helped carry into the derrick the bundle of bright tin tubes that had been lashed to a couple of curved iron supports at one side of the wagon. He also helped place in position the reel on which was wound two thousand feet of stout cord, by means of which the torpedo was to be let down into the well. This line was run through a pulley that hung directly above the well, and its end terminating in an iron hook, dangled close to the mouth of the deep, dark hole.

When these preparations were made, Brace Barlow began to fit and fasten together several lengths of small tin pipe until they formed a continuous tube about fifty feet long. This is called the "anchor," and was to be attached to the lower end of the shell, or large torpedo tube, so that when the whole was lowered into the well, it would support the torpedo at a height of fifty feet above the bottom.

Arthur was allowed to assist in fitting the anchor tubes, and also in making the shell ready to be filled with its deadly explosive. When the cans of nitroglycerine were brought into the derrick, all the men employed about the place retired to a respectful distance from it. Then Brace insisted that Arthur should also go away, and leave him alone to finish the delicate and dangerous job of loading the shell, lowering it into position, and exploding it.

The boy begged to be allowed to stay, declaring that he was not in the least afraid, and would keep as still as a mouse. But Brace would not listen for a moment to his pleadings, and very slowly the little fellow walked away to what he considered a safe distance, though it was not nearly so far as the men had gone.

At this time the empty shell, which was a large tin tube about twenty feet long, was, with its anchor attached, hanging in the well so that its upper end was just above the surface. It hung from a very shallow iron hook, at the end of the stout cord arranged for the purpose; and Brace Barlow now proceeded slowly and cautiously to pour the nitroglycerine into it. The stuff was the color of soft soap, and about as thick as syrup.

He had been thus engaged but a few minutes, when Arthur, who was nearer to him than anybody else, heard him call, "Come here, quick, somebody, and help me!"

Without a moment's hesitation or thought of fear, the brave little fellow ran swiftly to the derrick, exclaiming, as he reached it, "Here I am, Brace! What do you want?"

"You here, you dear little chap!" cried the torpedo man, "I did n't mean that you should come; but perhaps after all you will do better than another, and I must have help at once. You see the hook has slipped off the shell, and I only caught the torpedo in time to save it from dropping and exploding before I was ready. Then the weight of the cord pulled the hook up so that I can't reach it. Now if you can climb up the side of the derrick, holding the drill rope in close to you till you reach the proper height, then swing out, catch hold of that hook, and slide down the drill rope with it in your hand, you will do what I want as well as if you were the biggest man in the world. Do you think you can?"

"I can try," replied the boy, who took in the whole situation at a glance, and he at once began to climb the ladder that led to the top of the tall derrick.

It seemed that while Brace was filling the torpedo, and had nearly completed his task, he found it necessary to shift the position of the shell slightly. As he lifted it, the shallow hook slipped from the bail, or handle of stout copper wire, and flew up just beyond his reach. To let go of the torpedo was out of the question, for it would have fallen down the well and probably exploded from concussion with the iron tubing lining the hole before it had gone many feet. This explosion would have fired the quart or more of glycerine still remaining in one of the cans on the derrick floor, and Brace Barlow would instantly have disappeared from human view. The weight of the torpedo was so great that he could not support it very long; and so, unless assistance came to him promptly when he called, he must have let the thing drop, and suffered the consequences.

But help had come promptly; and a twelve-year-old boy, forgetting all thoughts of danger, and urged on by the love he bore his friend, was climbing the derrick, swinging out into space on the heavy drill rope, clutching the dangling iron hook, and sliding down with it in his hand. Then, instead of timidly reaching it to Brace, he stepped boldly up and attached it to the copper bail of the torpedo that was cutting deep into the flesh of the strong hand that held it, and must in another minute have let it go.

As the well-shooter, with a pale face, rose from his strained position, he clasped the boy in his arms, exclaiming: "Little one, you have done for me this day what any man might be proud of doing for a friend; and, so long as I live, I will never forget the service nor cease to be indebted to you."

When the filling of the torpedo was completed, it was cautiously lowered a thousand feet to the bottom of the well, the "Go Devil," a heavy, pointed bit of iron that was to explode it, was dropped, and, seizing Arthur in his arms, Brace Barlow ran swiftly from the spot.

A few seconds later the solid earth was shaken and there was a heavy but muffled roar. Directly afterwards a vast column of oil shot up through the derrick sixty feet into the air, and fell back to earth in a glistening cloud of amber-colored spray. The shot was a perfect success; and for months afterwards the old well again flowed at the rate of twenty barrels a day.

As Brace and his little friend rode homewards they stopped in the first lonely bit of forest to explode the still dangerous but empty nitro-glycerine cans. This was done by placing them on the ground, lighting the end of a short fuse attached to a cap thrust into one of them, and driving rapidly away. The explosion was terrific, and its roar was like that of a hundred-pounder gun. Arthur said it was better than any Fourth of July he had ever known.

CHAPTER V.

ARTHUR AND HIS COUSINS.

AS Arthur and Brace Barlow returned from the well-shooting described in the preceding chapter, the latter set the boy down at a cross-road but a short distance from the Dustin house. Here the little fellow bade his "dear giant" good-night, and ran homeward, feeling happier than he had for a long time. Though he hardly realized the full value of the service he had just rendered to his friend, he was sure that he had been useful at a critical moment; he knew that he had been praised for what he had done, and he felt more manly than ever before.

It was quite late when he reached the front gate, where faithful little Cynthia was anxiously watching for him and wondering where he could be.

"Oh, Cynthia!" he cried, as he drew near and saw her, "I've had such a lovely time! I have been shooting a well with Brace Barlow, and I climbed up the derrick and got a hook that had slipped away from him, and brought it down; and he said I was a brave boy, and had saved his life, though I don't see exactly how; and then we had a splendid Fourth of July time, blowing up the cans; and it sounded like a real truly cannon; and the very minute I get grown up I 'm going to be a well-shooter."

It was absolutely necessary for the enthusiastic little fellow to pour into sympathetic ear the tale of what he had done. He had performed a brave act, and in the first flush of his excitement he longed to be praised for it, as we all do whenever we have done anything that we consider especially good, or worthy of commendation. It is a reward of merit to which all who have earned it are entitled; and to withhold just praise is as cruel as to extend unjust censure.

Cynthia would not have been guilty of any such unkindness. Her eyes opened wide as she listened to the tale her Prince told of his own deeds, and she was just catching her breath to tell him how splendid she thought them, when they were startled by the sound of a harsh voice, calling, "Arthur! Cynthia! come into the house this minute, you naughty children. Don't you know better than to be staying out there breathing the night air?"

"A boy must breathe some kind of air, Aunt Nancy, and when it is night time I don't see how he can help breathing night air," laughed Arthur, as he reached the house; for not even his aunt's harsh tones could at once dispel his good spirits.

"What do you mean by talking back to me?" asked Mrs. Dustin. "I say that night air is poison, and no member of my family, even if he is a young interloper, shall breathe a drop of it, not so long as I can help it. Now, not another word. I know where you 've been this whole blessed afternoon. You 've been off with Brace Barlow, who ought to have more sense than to encourage your badness, shooting wells, and trying to get yourself blown into mince-meat, just to make more trouble for me. Yes, I know all about it, in spite of your sly ways. Now, you may go right to bed, and not a morsel of supper shall you have this night, which may be it 'll be a lesson that you will remember for one while, anyway."

Mr. John Dustin, who sat smoking his evening pipe by an open window, rarely interfered with his wife's management of the children; but now he spoke up saying:

"That won't do, wife; you only gave the boy bread and water for his dinner, and it won't do to send him to bed without any supper. I believe in proper punishment, where it is deserved, as much as anybody; but when it comes to starving, that's quite another thing. It shall never be said that my brother Richard's only son was starved in his uncle's house. So give the boy his supper, and plenty of it. Then you can send him to bed if you see fit."

Mrs. Dustin knew that when her husband spoke in this tone he meant to be obeyed; so, without a word, she set a plain but bountiful meal before Arthur. From a long experience of bread-and-water punishments and supperless nights the boy was wise enough to eat heartily all that he possibly could, in spite of his heavy heart. He ate in silence, and for some time nobody else spoke; only Dick, who sat at the farther end of the room with the other children, chuckled and made faces behind Arthur's back, for the benefit, and to the huge delight, of his companions. He was greatly pleased at the result of his tale-bearing; for it was he who, overhearing Arthur tell Cynthia that he had been well-shooting with Brace Barlow, had hurried to the house, and repeated the information, with some picturesque additions of his own devising, to his mother.

Once, during the silent meal, little Cynthia tried to create a diversion in her cousin's favor by remarking timidly to nobody in particular, but to the company in general, "Arthur says Brace Barlow says he saved his life."

"Who says what?" inquired Mrs. Dustin, turning quickly and fixing her sharp eyes on the little girl's face.

"Brace Barlow says—I mean Arthur says Brace Barlow says—he saved his——"

"Oh, fiddlesticks!" interrupted her mother; "you don't know what you're talking about. It is n't at all likely that either of them did anything of the kind. The sort of danger Brace Barlow goes into is quick and sure. When it once gets started there is n't any chance for life-saving, or for telling of it afterwards. Arthur ought to know better than to go round boasting in that way to a little girl like you, and I should think he 'd be ashamed of himself for doing it."

Arthur listened to this unjust speech with a flushed face and a feeling of choking indignation; but he did not say a word. Young as he was, he had already learned that in a contest with an unreasonable person silence is the weapon of wisdom.

After finishing his supper the forlorn little fellow, accepting his punishment without a murmur, though he could not imagine what wrong he had done, retired to his cot in the wood-shed, where he was quickly blessed by the presence of sleep the comforter.

The next day was the bright one in September with which this story opens, and Arthur is introduced as he sits on the top rail of a zig-zag fence watching the other children at play.

Fired by the accounts of his adventure of the day before as narrated to them, at second-hand by Cynthia, for Arthur could not be induced to say another word concerning it, his cousins had determined to have a miniature well-shooting of their own. They spent the entire morning in the construction of a very shaky little derrick, about six feet high, and now they were busy drilling a well, which they hoped to put down to a depth of at least two feet. When it was finished they proposed to shoot it by means of a cannon cracker, that they had saved over from the Fourth of July for use on some such special occasion.

The scheme was well planned, and seemed likely to be carried out; for the children were enthusiastic over it, and, under Dick's direction, worked most diligently. Arthur would gladly have joined in this fascinating occupation; but the others would not have him. As Dick scornfully remarked: "What can a city chap like you know about building derricks and drilling wells? You was n't raised in the oil region."

So Arthur was forced to content himself with sitting on the fence and watching them. Occasionally he turned for a chat with Uncle Phin, who was cutting brush in the field behind him, and who took a long rest whenever he reached the end of a row that brought him anywhere near his "lil marse." Finally, after one of these rests, during which Arthur had paid no attention to the operations at the miniature derrick, he left his perch and followed Uncle Phin for a short distance into the thick brush.

CHAPTER VI.

A GALLANT RESCUE AND ITS REWARD.

ARTHUR had hardly left his perch before he was startled by a perfect babel of sounds coming from where the children were at play. There were yells and shouts of laughter, mingled with cries of pain and an angry screaming, together with piteous calls of "Arthur! oh, Arthur! Come and make 'em stop!"

Like a young deer the boy bounded out of the brush and over the fence, followed, much more slowly by Uncle Phin. Arrived upon the scene, he quickly comprehended the situation. In an unfortunate moment, just as the well was completed and ready to be shot, Cynthia's dearly loved little white kitty came demurely walking in that direction looking for her mistress. At sight of the little animal a brilliant idea flashed through Dick's mind, and he at once proceeded to carry it out. He said:

"We can't have much fun shooting a dry well anyhow, 'cause there won't be any oil to fly up in the air; but I'll tell you what. Let's have an execution by 'lectricity. It'll be immense, and here's the prisoner already waiting to be executed."

Thus saying, the cruel boy snatched up the little white kitty, and, bidding the others hold Cynthia, who was ready to make a furious struggle in defence of her pet, he ran with it to the derrick. Here, with the make-believe drill rope, he hung it by the tail, so that the little pink nose was but a few inches from the ground. Then, lighting the fuse of the great cannon-cracker, he placed it directly beneath the victim, who was now uttering piteous cries of pain and terror, and ran to where the others were shouting with delight over the new and thrilling diversion so unexpectedly prepared for them.

Poor, desperate little Cynthia, kicking, biting, scratching, but struggling in vain with the young rascals who held her fast, began, as a last resort, to call upon Arthur, the brave Prince who had defended her against the big dog, and she did not call in vain.

Hatless and breathless, with the fire of righteous wrath blazing in his blue eyes, the plucky boy came flying to the rescue. He had no thought of the overwhelming odds against him. The princes of his fairy tales fought whole armies single-handed, and why should not he? His impetuous speed carried him right through the shouting group assembled to witness the execution of the hapless kitty, and two of them were flung to the ground before they knew of his presence. An instant later he reached the little derrick. The fuse had burned down into the body of the big cracker, and in another second it would explode. Without the faintest trace of hesitation, the little fellow seized it and flung it behind him.

An explosion followed almost instantly, and was accompanied by a yell of pain. The moment Dick recognized Arthur, and perceived his intention, he sprang after his cousin, and was directly in line when the cannon-cracker came flying toward him. It struck him and fell to the ground, exploding as it did so, and burning his bare feet painfully.

Furious with rage the cowardly young bully rushed at Arthur, who was releasing the white kitty from her unhappy position, and with a savage blow knocked the little fellow down. Then he jumped on him and began to pummel him, screaming "Take that, will you! And that! I'll teach you! I'll show you who's boss round here!"

All at once these cruel cries were changed to yells of dismay, as, whack! whack! whack! a shower of stinging blows fell upon Dick's shoulders. Uncle Phin, who had followed Arthur as fast as he was able, had arrived just in time to save his "lil Marse" from any severe injury at the hands of his enraged cousin, and to administer, with a stout stick, the thrashing that the young rascal so well deserved.

In less than a minute cowardly Cousin Dick and his frightened followers were scampering away towards the house, where they proposed to lay their side of the case promptly before their mother. Cynthia had gone after her beloved kitty, and brave little "Prince Dusty," who had flung himself into Uncle Phin's arms, was sobbing as though his heart would break.

"Soh, Honey, soh, don't you cry now," murmured the old man, in soothing tones. "'Member dat while you is a Dustin by name, you 's a Dale by breedin, an comes of Dale stock. You 's mos a man now, a young gen'lm'n, an it won't nebber do fer sich as you is to cry like a lilly gal. Soh, now, Honey, soh."

Neither of them heard the quick, determined step that approached them from behind, and so occupied was poor, troubled Uncle Phin in soothing and comforting his charge, that it was an easy matter for Mrs. Dustin to snatch the trembling boy from his arms. Then she marched rapidly away, without a word; but dragging her victim relentlessly after her.

Uncle Phin half started to his feet when he first realized what was happening; but sank back again with a groan, and a murmured "De good Lawd hab mussy on His Lamb."

Then he bowed his frosted head on his knees and the hot tears trickled slowly between his black fingers.

While he thus sat helpless and despairing, poor Arthur was taken to the house and there whipped, until the apple-tree switch broke, and his Aunt Nancy's strength was exhausted. Then, telling the boy that this was a lesson for him to remember as long as he lived, she bade him go to the woodshed, which was his sleeping-room, and stay there until she should release him.

During this undeserved punishment not a cry had escaped from the boy, nor had a tear found its way to his eyes. He bit his under-lip and clenched his hands, but not a sound did he utter. He remembered what Uncle Phin had just told him. He was almost a man now, and no man, especially a Dale, would cry for a whipping. So, though the little face was drawn and white, and the boy trembled until he could hardly stand, he held out to the end as bravely as ever a martyr under torture, and when he was thrust into his cheerless shed, he sat on the edge of his rude bed rigid and tearless. His mind was in a furious whirl, but above all was the overwhelming sense of injustice and outrage.

Finally he sprang to his feet, crying, "I hate you! I hate you! I hate you!" and then, flinging himself on his bed, he gave way to a burst of passionate weeping.

"Oh, mamma!" he cried, "my own mamma! why don't you come for me and take me away from this dreadful place? I can't stay here any longer! Indeed I can't, mamma! oh, come for me; do come! Please, mamma, come for me, and take me to where you are!"

For nearly an hour the forlorn child cried for the dear ones who had left him; then his sobs gradually died away, and, utterly exhausted, he fell into a troubled sleep.

In the meantime little Cynthia, who only found her dear kitty after a long search, met her father coming home from his work, and when he inquired what was the matter with his daughter, and who had made her cry, she told him the truth of all that had happened, so far as she knew it. Mr. Dustin had begun to suspect that Arthur was ill-treated by his cousins, and as he listened to Cynthia's story, his face grew very stern, and he said: "This matter must be looked into."

When they reached the house, and he was told that Arthur had been severely punished for trying to kill Cynthia's kitten, and for fighting with Dick who had rescued it, and that Uncle Phin had beaten Dick, Mr. Dustin's anger could not be restrained. He said:

"Wife, I am afraid you have made a terrible mistake, and punished an innocent child for performing a noble act. If what Cynthia tells me is true, and I believe it is, Master Dick is the boy who tormented his little sister, and would have killed her pet. Master Dick is the coward who thrashed a little fellow two years younger than himself, for bravely rescuing the victim of his cruelty. Master Dick is the one who told a lie to hide his own wickedness and cause his cousin to receive the punishment he himself deserved. And Master Dick is the boy who is aching for the whipping that I shall give him before he is many minutes older.

"In regard to my dead brother's child, I want it understood that so long as he remains under my roof he is never again to be punished for any fault, real or fancied; and if anybody has any complaints to make against him, they must make them to me. As for Uncle Phin, if it is true that he beat one of my children, he must leave this place, and look for a home elsewhere, which I shall tell him to-morrow."

Every word of this was heard by the old negro, who was sitting on a bench in the little vine-colored porch, close under an open window, of the room in which Mr. Dustin stood. The old man, who had not known of the cruel punishment inflicted upon his "lil Marse," was waiting patiently for Arthur to come out and bring him his supper, as the boy had done every evening since they came there to live.

Now he said to himself: "Dat's all right, Marse

Dustin. I did beat yo boy, an I do it agin if heem tetch my honey lamb; but yo sha'n't nebber hab de chance to tun ole Phin Dale from yo house. No, sah; he done go of his own sef, befo ebber he 'lowin you to do sich a ting. An when he go he is n't gwine erlone. No, sah."

Just then little Cynthia came out with his supper, and said that Arthur was asleep. The old man ate his frugal meal in silence; but a train of thoughts was passing through his head much more rapidly than usual. They were all travelling in the same direction, and it was back toward his old Virginia home.

CHAPTER VII.

UNCLE PHIN'S PLAN.

AFTER finishing his supper on the memorable evening of Arthur's unjust punishment, Mr. John Dustin stepped softly into the woodshed, which, in that overcrowded household, had seemed to be the only place that could be given up for an extra sleeping-room. He closed the door behind him, and, by the light of a candle that he carried, gazed long and earnestly at the tear-stained face of the child who lay on a rude cot. It was hot and flushed, and the sleeping boy tossed and moaned as though visited by unhappy dreams. Once he called out: "Don't let them whip me, mamma! I have n't been naughty. Indeed I have not!"

At this the man, as though fearful of awakening the sleeper, hastily retired from the place, and there was a suspicious moisture in his eyes as he re-entered the other room.

Here he said: "Wife, I believe we have treated that little chap very unjustly. My brother Richard was the most truthful and honorable boy and man I ever knew, and I am inclined to think the son takes after his father. Hereafter I shall try to make his life pleasanter and happier, and in this I want you to help me."

Mrs. Dustin made no answer to this, for her heart was hardened against the orphan lad, and she really believed him to be the sly bad boy that Dick strove to make him appear. "I will watch him more closely than ever, and show him up in his true light yet," she thought, as she bent her head over her sewing so that her husband could not see her face. "He sha'n't stand in the way of my children, and I'll believe my own Dick's word before his every time," was her mental resolve.

Knowing nothing of his wife's thoughts, Mr. Dustin was already taking steps to insure Arthur's greater comfort. He went to the pantry and brought from it a bowl of milk, a loaf of new bread, and a plate of ginger cookies made that day. With these he again entered Arthur's sleeping-room, and softly placed them on a chair where, by the light of the moon that was just rising, the boy would see them whenever he should awake. Once, while he was thus engaged, Mrs. Dustin opened her mouth to remonstrate against such a lavish provision of food for a mere child; but a glance at her husband's determined face caused her to change her mind, and she wisely remained silent.

There had been another and more appreciative witness of Mr. Dustin's thoughtful act. It was Uncle Phin, who, kneeling outside the shed and gazing through an open chink in its rough wall, was waiting patiently for the family to retire that he might have a private and undetected conversation with his "lil Marse."

As Mr. Dustin again left the shed, the old man said softly to himself:

"De good Lawd bress you fer what you is jes done, Marse Dustin. You is got some ob pore Marse Richard's goodness into you after all. If it warn't fer de ole Miss an dem wicked chillun, me an lil Marse would try an stick it out awhile longer. But it can't be did. No, sah, it can't be did." Here the old man shook his white head sorrowfully. "Dem young limbs is too powerful wicked, an ole

Miss, she back 'em up. Fer a fac, ole Phin got ter tote his lamb away fum heah, an maybe de good Lawd lead us to de green fiels ob de still waters, where we kin lie down in peacefulness."

An hour later, when the lights of the house were extinguished and all was still with the silence of sleep, Uncle Phin cautiously opened the shed door, and tip-toeing heavily to where Arthur lay, rested his horny hand gently on the boy's white forehead.

The child opened his eyes and smiled, as, by the moonlight, now flooding the place, he saw who was bending over him.

"Sh-h-h, Honey," whispered Uncle Phin, with warning finger uplifted; "git up quiet like a fiel mouse an come erlong wif me. Sh-h-h!"

Then the old man and the child stole softly away, the former not forgetting to carry with him the supply of food provided by Mr. Dustin. As quietly as two shadows they moved across the open space between the house and the barn.

Not until they were safe in his particular corner of the hay-mow did Uncle Phin venture to speak aloud. Here he drew a long breath of satisfaction, for in this place they could talk freely and without danger of being overheard.

First he made Arthur drink all that he could from the bowl of milk and eat heartily of the bread and cakes that Mr. Dustin had left for him. After eating the food, of which he stood so greatly in need, and which the old man assured him had been left by one "ob de good Lawd's own rabens," Arthur said:

"Oh, Uncle Phin, I've tried as hard as I can to be good, and make them all love me here, but they won't do it. No matter what I do, it seems to be the wrong thing, and I only get punished for it. I am getting almost afraid to try and do right any more, and if we stay here much longer I'm pretty sure I shall grow to be a bad boy, such as my own dear mamma and papa would n't love. Now don't you think we might run away and live somewhere else, where it would be more easy to be good than it is here? Do you think it would be very wrong if we did? I'm sure Aunt Nancy would be glad to have us go, and perhaps Uncle John would too."

"Why, Honeybug!" cried the old man delightedly, "dat ar is prezactly what yo ole Unc Phin's been projeckin to hissef—only you mus'n't call it

runnin away, like you was a pore niggah. A Dale
don't nebber run away. He only change de spere
ob his libbin, when he gits tired ob one place, an'
takes up wif anudder, same like we 's a gwine ter.
I 's been considerin fer a long while back dat dese
yere Dustins, who is n't much better 'n pore white
trash no how, was n't de bestest company fer a
thorobred Dale like you is."

"Hush, Uncle Phin! You must not speak so of
my uncle's family. He was my dear papa's own
brother, and they are the only relatives I have in the
world," said Arthur.

"No, dey is n't, Honey. Dey is n't de onliest ones
what you got in de worl. You is got a granpaw
libin yet. A monsrus fine gen'lm'n he is, and he's
place one ob de fines' in all Ferginny, if I does say it.
He 's quality, he is, an Dalecourt is yo own proper-
est home."

"But I have never seen my Grandpapa Dale, and
he does n't know me, and I don't believe he wants
to," replied Arthur; adding sadly: "There does n't
seem to be anybody in the whole world that wants
to know me, except you, and Brace Barlow, and
Cynthia. Besides Dalecourt is a long way off, and

it would take a great deal of money to get there, and we have n't any at all, and I don't believe even you could find the way to it if we should try and go there."

"Dint I uster lib dere, Honey, and dint I come frum dere? What fo you spec I can't go whar I come frum?"

"But coming from a place and going back to it are very different things," replied Arthur, wisely.

"So dey is, Honey, ob cose dey is," agreed Uncle Phin, who was not yet ready to disclose his plans.

"But we will go away somewhere and live together, won't we?" pleaded Arthur. "I don't suppose we could take my 'dear Giant' and Cynthia with us; but if we only could, would n't we be happy?"

"Ob cose we'se a gwine leab dish yere place," replied the old man. "You jes trus yo Unc Phin, an he fin a way to trabble, an a place fer to go."

Then he told the boy that he should go away before daylight, and might remain several days making preparations for their journey. He would not say where he was going, because he wanted Arthur to be able to say honestly he did not know, if he were asked. He instructed the boy to collect all his little belongings, including his scanty wardrobe, and have them ready for a start at a moment's notice. "It 'll be in de night time, Honey, in de middle ob de night, an ole Phin 'll creep in an wake you, same like he did erwhile ago. So don't you be afeared when you wakes up sudden an fin's him stan'in alongside ob you."

"No, I won't be afraid, and I 'll be ready whenever you come for me," replied the little fellow; "but don't stay long away, because I shall be so lonely without you."

Uncle Phin promised that he would not be a single minute longer than was necessary to make preparations, and Arthur was about to go back to the house, when a sudden thought flashed into his mind, and he exclaimed: "Oh, my book, my precious book that the beautiful lady gave me! I can't leave it behind, and I 'm afraid Aunt Nancy won't let me have it."

Then, in answer to Uncle Phin's inquiries, he had to tell him the whole story of his adventures as a Prince, which he had not heretofore found an opportunity of relating, and in which the old man was greatly interested. He was particularly pleased with the title bestowed upon his "lil Marse" by the beautiful lady, and said: "You is a shuah 'nough Prince, Honey, if dere ebber was one in dis worl, only you won't always be Prince Dusty. Some day you'll be a Prince somefin else. But you mus hab yo book, in cose you mus, an we'll make out to git hol ob it somehow or nudder."

Comforted by this assurance, and filled with the new hopes raised by their prolonged conversation, Arthur flung his arms about the old man's neck and kissed him good-night and good-bye. Then slipping from the hay-mow he sped back to the house, carrying the empty dishes, from which Uncle Phin had taken the remnants of food for his own use.

CHAPTER VIII.

AWAKENED AT MIDNIGHT.

THE next morning Mrs. Dustin was greatly surprised on coming down stairs to find that no fire had been made in the kitchen stove, and that the water-buckets, standing on a shelf over the sink, were empty. Nothing of this kind had happened since Arthur and Uncle Phin came there to live, nearly two months before; for to light the fire and bring fresh water into the house were among the very first of Uncle Phin's morning duties. Arthur had meant to get up very early this morning and do these things, with a vague hope that the old negro's absence might not be noticed; but he was so thoroughly exhausted by the events of the preceding day and night, that he overslept and only awoke with a start as his Aunt Nancy entered the kitchen.

Now, wide-awake, the boy lay trembling in bed and wondered what would happen. He heard his aunt go out to the barn and call "Phin! Uncle Phin!" but there was no answer, though the call was repeated several times. Then she came back muttering something about "lazy and worthless old niggers," and Arthur heard her making the fire. Still anxious to take Uncle Phin's place as far as possible, he jumped up, and hastily slipping on his ragged clothes, picked up an armful of wood that he carried into the kitchen.

His aunt looked at him sharply: "Where is Phin?" she demanded.

"I do not know," answered the boy.

"Humph! I might have expected you would say that," she replied. "How did you know I wanted any wood, then?"

"I heard you calling Uncle Phin, and thought perhaps that was what you wanted him for," was the reply.

"Well, then, if you know so well what I want, perhaps you know that I want you to get out of this kitchen and keep out of the way while I am getting breakfast," said Mrs. Dustin, angrily.

It is always those whom we have injured the most that we dislike the most; and, with the recollection of her cruelty toward this gentle child fresh in her mind, the mere sight of him filled her with anger.

So the little fellow wandered out to the barn, and felt very lonely as he climbed up on the hay-mow to make sure that his dearest earthly friend had indeed gone. He sat down to wonder where Uncle Phin was, and how long it would be before he would come to take him away from that unhappy place. He wished that he might stay right where he was, and not be compelled to see any of the family again, and was feeling very wretched and forlorn generally. All at once he heard Cynthia's voice calling the chickens around her on the barn floor where she fed them every morning. Here was somebody for whom he cared, and the thought that he was so soon to leave her, probably forever, filled him with a pang of mingled pain and love.

He slid down from the hay-mow to where his little cousin stood, and as she threw her arms about his neck and kissed him and told him how much she loved him and how sorry she was for him, he began to realize how hard it would be to part from her, and to wonder if after all he ought to run away with Uncle Phin.

Cynthia was a loving and lovable little soul, and though she had a freckled face, it was lighted by a pair of glorious brown eyes. Her hair was of a rich brown, flecked with specks of red gold where the sunlight shone through it. It was just such hair as the sun loves to kiss, and the merry wind delighted to toss it into the most bewitching tangles whenever it was not closely imprisoned under the little pink sun-bonnet. It reminded Arthur of his own dear mother's hair, and often when they were playing together he would snatch off the pink sun-bonnet just for the pleasure of seeing it ripple down over her shoulders. His own used to be long, almost as long as Cynthia's, but his Aunt Nancy had cut it off when he first came to live there, and it had been clipped short ever since, greatly to Uncle Phin's sorrow.

While Arthur and Cynthia were feeding the chickens, and the former was almost forgetting his recent loneliness, Mr. Dustin came into the barn. He greeted both the children pleasantly, and even kissed them, a thing that Arthur wondered at, for he could not remember that it had ever happened before. Then he asked, "Do you know where Uncle Phin is, Arthur?"

"I think he has gone away," replied the boy, flushing and looking down, for it seemed somehow as though he were not exactly telling the truth.

"Do you know where he has gone?"

"No, sir, I do not," was the honest reply, and the boy looked his questioner squarely in the face as he made it.

"Well, I believe you, of course," said his uncle, "and I suppose he must have taken it into his head to leave us, though it seems very strange that he should have done so without bidding you good-bye, or telling you where he was going."

This was too much for Arthur's sense of honor, and speaking up manfully, he said: "He did tell me he was going away, Uncle John, and bid me good-bye but he did n't tell me where he was going, and he did n't want me to say anything about it unless I had to."

"I am glad you have told me this," said Mr. Dustin, "and since he has gone I must say I am not very sorry. Now come in to breakfast."

That morning Mr. Dustin took Arthur and Cynthia with him to the well he was drilling, and, to their great delight, allowed them to stay there all day. When they reached home that evening Arthur was so emboldened by his uncle's unusual kindness, that he ventured, in his presence, to make mention of the book of fairy tales that his Aunt Nancy had taken from him. He said:

"Is n't the book the beautiful lady gave me my very own, Aunt Nancy?"

"I suppose it is," answered Mrs. Dustin, shortly.

"Well, then, don't you think I might have it just to look at?"

"I said you might have it when I got ready to give it to you."

Then Mr. Dustin inquired what book they referred to, and when it was explained to him he said:

"Well, I guess your aunt is ready to let you have it this very minute, are n't you, wife?"

"There was no mistaking his meaning; and, very ungraciously, Aunt Nancy took the precious book down from its high shelf and tossed it on the table.

Arthur seized it eagerly, and until the children were sent to bed they and Mr. Dustin enjoyed looking at its many beautiful illustrations. That night Arthur slept with it under his pillow and it must have influenced his dreams for they were very pleasant ones.

The following day was also a happy one for Arthur and Cynthia, for they spent most of it sitting close together under the roots of the great overturned tree that was their especial retreat absorbed in the book, and discussing, in their wise childish way, several of its charming stories that Arthur read aloud to his little cousin.

The boy was beginning to think that life in this place was not so very cheerless after all, and was becoming more than ever doubtful of the expediency of running away, when an incident took place that restored all his previous resolves. Cynthia had been called in by her mother to sew on her hated patchwork, and Arthur was sitting alone, when suddenly a great, squirming, half-dead snake was dropped on him from above. With a cry of horror the startled boy sprang up just in time to see his Cousin Dick's grinning face, and hear him say, "That's only part of what you'll get before long, you little sneak, you."

That night as he slept with his precious book clasped tightly in his arms, he was again awakened by a hand laid lightly on his forehead. As he sprang to a sitting posture, Uncle Phin bent lovingly over him, saying:

"Sh-h-h, Honey! Ebberyting 's ready, an it 's high time fer us to be gittin away frum hyar."

CHAPTER IX.

A HURRIED FLIGHT.

THERE was no need for Arthur to ask any questions, when he was roused in the middle of the second night after Uncle Phin's departure. He realized at once what was required of him, and the heaviness of sleep instantly vanished, leaving him keenly wide awake. Stepping softly from his bed, he quickly dressed, while the old negro gathered together everything belonging to his "lil Marse," and placed the things in a corn-sack that he had brought for that purpose.

"Is dat yo book, Honey?" he whispered, noticing the volume of fairy tales lying on the bed.

"Yes, that is my own precious book that the beautiful lady gave me; but don't put it in the bag, Uncle Phin, I want to carry it myself."

Then the thoughtful little fellow, since he could not bid Cynthia good-bye, and feared she might feel hurt if he went away without a word, begged his companion to wait, just a minute, while he wrote her a note. He wrote it by the bright moonlight, on a bit of brown paper, with the stump of a lead-pencil, so that it was not a very elegant production, but it answered its purpose, and was tenderly cherished for many a day by the little girl who received it the next morning. In it, in a big, scrawling hand, was written :

"Dear Cynthia : I have been so much trouble here, specially to Aunt Nancy and Dick, that I am going away with uncle Fin, to find another home. I love you dearly, and sometime I hope I shall come back and see you. Good-bye, from
"Your loving cousin,
"Arthur."

Although the old negro was in a hurry to be off, he waited patiently while Arthur slowly wrote this note. To him writing was one of the most mysterious and difficult of arts ; and, gazing admiringly at the young penman, he murmured to himself :

"What a fine lilly gen'l'man him be to be shuah. Him only twelve year ole ; but settin dar an er writin like he was a hundred."

When the note was finished it was pinned to the pillow of the cot-bed, and, with a lingering look at the place that had sheltered him for a year, the child stepped out and softly closed the door. Then clasping his precious book tightly under his arm, and trustingly following the old negro, Arthur started on the wonderful journey that was to change the whole course of his life, though he was still ignorant of their destination.

When they were safely behind the barn, out of sight and hearing of the house, Uncle Phin stopped and said :

"Dere's only one ting trubblin dis yeah ole woolly head. Kin you tell, Honey, fer shuah, what way de ribber ober yander is a runnin'?"

"Which, the Alleghany? Why, south, of course," answered Arthur, wondering at the question.

"Dat's what I lowed it done!" exclaimed the old man. "I knowed it didn' run yeast, kase dat ar way de sun rise, and I knowed it didn' run wes, kase dat ar way him a settin; but I wasn' rightly shuah him didn' run to de norf. I was figgerin all de time dough on him running to de souf, an now we'm git back to ole Ferginny easy an sartin."

"To Virginia!" cried Arthur, in dismay. "Are we going to try and go way to Virginia, Uncle Phin?"

"Ob cose we is, Honey. We'se er gwine to Ferginny, an Dalecourt, an yo granpaw, an de lil ole cabin by the magnole tree. We is gwine to yo own shuah 'nough home, Honey."

"But how are we ever going to travel so far?"

"You'll see, Honey! you'll see dreckly," chuckled the other. "I 'se got a great 'sprise in sto fer you. Hyar's de kerridge a waitin on us now, and Misto Barlow is gwine dribe us to the steamboat."

They were now on the road, at some distance from the house, and as Uncle Phin spoke, Arthur saw, drawn up to one side in the shadow of a clump of trees, Brace Barlow's team, and, leaning against the light wagon, the young man himself.

"Oh, Brace!" he cried, springing forward the moment he saw who it was, "I 'm so glad! I did n't want to go away without seeing you again. Are you really going with us?"

"I wish I could go with you all the way, my boy, and see you safe to your journey's end, but you know I can't leave my old mother. So I am only going to give you a lift for a little way and see that you get a good start. Jump in quick now for we've got a long drive ahead of us and I must be back by daylight."

As the spirited horses dashed away over the moonlit road with Arthur nestled between Brace and Uncle Phin on the single seat of the wagon, the boy learned how it happened that his friend had been induced to aid them in their flight. Uncle Phin had gone directly to him two nights before, and roused his indignation by describing the unhappy life his young charge was leading, and how much he suffered at the hands of Mrs. Dustin and her children. Then he told Brace of Dalecourt, and gave him to understand that Colonel Dale was ready to receive his grandson with open arms, whenever he should go to him.

The kind-hearted young fellow, entertaining a sincere regard for the little chap who had recently rendered him so great a service, readily agreed to a plan that promised so much of good to the boy, and willingly consented to assist him and Uncle Phin to make a start on their journey. He devoted two whole days to the task of preparing for it, and did so much more than Uncle Phin had dared ask or hope for, as

A HURRIED FLIGHT BY MOONLIGHT. (*Page* 70.)

to win the old man's everlasting gratitude and render the first stage of their journey comparatively easy.

For some time Arthur enjoyed the exciting night ride over the steep mountain roads, across deep valleys, and through forests, all bathed in the glorious, unclouded moonlight. He did not ask whither he was being taken. Nestled warmly between his two best friends he felt perfectly safe and happy. He knew that they would do what was best for him, and the very mystery and uncertainty attending this part of their journey lent it a fascination. At length his weary head nodded, the heavy eyelids closed, and, sound asleep, he was unconscious of his surroundings until the horses stopped, and he awoke to find himself being lifted from the wagon.

There was a gleam of moonlit water in his eyes, and as he dimly realized that he was on the bank of a river, strong arms bore him into the cabin of a queer-looking craft that lay moored to the forest trees. Here the boy was gently laid down, and was vaguely conscious that Brace Barlow was bidding him good-bye, when the sleepy eyelids again closed and the child passed into dream-land.

The young man stood looking at the sleeping boy for a full minute. As he did so he said softly: "Dear little chap! I hate to have you go away, and to think I may never see you again. But I suppose it's the best thing to be done, or I would n't have lifted a hand to help it along. I only hope it will come out all right, and that you'll have a happier life in the place you're going to than you ever could have had here. God bless you."

It was a benediction, as well as the farewell of one brave soul to another. As he uttered it the young man slipped a bank bill between two pages of the book the boy had clasped so closely, but which had now fallen from his hands.

"It's little enough," he said to himself as he turned away, "but it's all I've got, and may be it will help him out of a fix some time." Then he went out to assist Uncle Phin, who was casting off the fastenings of the boat, and preparing to push it from the shore.

In another minute the clumsy old craft had swung clear of the bank, and was moving slowly down stream in the shadow of the great trees that grew to the water's edge. Brace Barlow watched it until it became a part of the shadows, and he could no longer distinguish the white-headed figure bending over the long sweep that was made to do duty as a steering oar or rudder. Then he again mounted the seat of his light wagon, and started on his long homeward drive, feeling more lonely than he had ever felt in all his life.

CHAPTER X.

ON BOARD THE ARK.

THE craft on which the old man and the sleeping boy were now slowly drifting down the broad, moonlit stream, was a tiny house-boat, such as are common on all American rivers. It had floated down, empty and ownerless, with the high waters of the preceding spring, and had stranded and been left by the receding flood at the point where Uncle Phin discovered it some weeks before. It was a small, flat-bottomed scow, on which was built a low house, ten feet long and six wide. This house contained but a single room; and beyond it, at either end, the deck of the scow projected about four feet. At each end of the house was a door, and on each side a square hole or window, that closed with a wooden shutter.

At the stern was a steering oar, as has been stated. It hung on a swivel and its long handle projected up over the end of the roof, on which the steersman stood. From each side of the roof hung a heavy sweep, by means of which the craft might be slowly propelled or turned in any desired direction. When not in use, the lower ends of these could be lifted from the water by ropes attached to their blades, and fastened to the sides of the house. A rude ladder reached from each of the small end decks to the top of the roof. The whole affair was strong and in good condition, but rough and unpainted.

When it came down with the flood and stranded on the river bank, it contained nothing in the shape of furniture, save a couple of bunks built against the sides, the same number of rough benches, and several shelves put up here and there in convenient corners.

Uncle Phin had not thought of making use of this stranded craft, when he first found it among the trees that he was marking to be cut down for firewood. He slept in it one night, and merely regarded it as a convenient shelter that he could occupy when working in that distant and lonely place. When, however, he and Arthur conceived the idea of running away, and he made up his mind that if they did, it must be to travel in the direction of Dalecourt, a vision of the little old house-boat crossed his mind.

If it could only be got into the water, and should prove to be tight and sound, how easy and pleasant it would be to float down the river in it. Whenever they had gone as far as they saw fit by water, they could probably sell the boat for enough money to meet their expenses on the rest of the journey. It seemed a fine scheme, and Uncle Phin hastened to lay it before Brace Barlow and ask his advice concerning it.

The young man listened to it with great interest, and then they drove over to take a look at the stranded craft. After a careful examination, Brace said that, with a little calking of its seams, the boat could be made tight and river-worthy, and that Uncle Phin's plan seemed to him a first-class one. He furthermore offered his own labor and the use of his team to help prepare the craft for its voyage, and get it once more afloat.

This offer was thankfully accepted, and the two succeeding days had been busy ones for both men and horses. It was found necessary to make several trips back and forth between Brace Barlow's house and the "Ark," as he called the boat. Then they calked her open seams, and smeared them thickly with pitch. They constructed a rude track of straight young tree-trunks, from the boat to the water, into which, aided by rollers, long levers, and the horses, they finally succeeded in launching her. After this they had the sweeps to make, and, as there was no stove, Uncle Phin built a fire-place in the middle of the floor, near one end of the cabin. This he did by forming a square of large rocks, filling it with small stones, and covering the whole with a thick layer of earth. They filled the bunks with sweet, fresh straw, and made pillows of the flour sacks stuffed with the same material. Brace Barlow covered one of these bunks with a coarse sheet and a blanket drawn from his own slender stock of household goods. Uncle Phin had his own bedding, that consisted of a thin old army blanket and a tattered comforter. He also had an axe, which was the only piece of valuable property that he possessed.

Then Brace Barlow bought several cooking utensils, a few dishes, and a small supply of provisions, to which he added potatoes and a dozen eggs from his own little farm.

When all this had been accomplished, the two men surveyed their work with great satisfaction, and nothing but his duty to his mother prevented Brace Barlow from joining the party and making the voyage down the river with them.

From information furnished by Uncle Phin the young man gained an idea that the greater part of their journey was to be performed by water, and that Dalecourt was somewhere in West Virginia, within a few miles of the point to which the ark could be navigated.

This was also Uncle Phin's idea when he learned that the river on which his craft was launched flowed into the Ohio, which in turn washed one of the borders of West Virginia. This new name meant nothing to him. There had been but one Virginia when he left it, and even of its extent he had not the slightest conception. He imagined that, once within the borders of the State, it would be a simple matter to discover and reach his old home. All he knew of travelling and distances was, that when he followed his young mistress to New York, the journey occupied less than two days, and that the one from New York to the oil country had been accomplished in about the same space of time. So now, while he was well aware that a boat, drifting with the current, would not travel quite as fast as a train of cars, he did not, for a moment, doubt that two or three weeks or a month at the very most, would see them safely established beneath the stately magnolias of Dalecourt.

Had he known that between the place where they must leave their boat and their destination, there stretched a weary distance of nearly five hundred miles, much of which was across rugged mountain ranges, it is probable that even his stout heart would have shrunk from so great an undertaking. But he had no knowledge of this, and, as happily ignorant of what was before them as was his beloved "lil Marse," now sleeping so peacefully on his bed of straw, the old man floated contentedly over the gleaming waters, and recalled bright pictures of the dear old home he hoped so soon to see.

The night was far advanced; he was worn out with the fatiguing labor of the preceding two days, there was no sound to disturb him, and so, after a while, his head sunk low over the steering oar, and ere long he too was fast asleep.

Thus, with no wakeful eye to determine her course, the Ark drifted on through the night; now in deep shadows of great hills or dark forests, then across long stretches of silvery moonlight; here caught by an eddy and turned slowly round and round; there held for a moment on the point of some glistening sand-bar from which she would slowly swing off and again move ahead.

While the occupants of the boat still slept, the moonlight paled before the rosy dawn of a new day, and at last a mischievous beam from the round red sun, just peeping over the eastern hills, found its way into the little cabin and shone full across Arthur's eyes. In a moment the boy was wide-awake, and gazing upon his strange surroundings with the utmost bewilderment. He heard no sound, perceived no motion, and had not the faintest idea that he was on a boat. He only wondered whose this strange house was, where it was, and what had become of Uncle Phin, of whom he could see no sign.

He almost expected to hear his Aunt Nancy's harsh voice calling him. Then the events of the preceding night came slowly back to him; and, with a thrill of joy he remembered that he was far from her dreaded presence, and had actually started on a journey toward his own dear mother's beautiful home.

But he must get up and find out where he was, and what had become of Brace Barlow and Uncle Phin. At the very moment he stepped from his straw-filled bunk there came a crash and a shock that flung him to the floor. At the same instant he heard a frightened cry and a loud splash. Regaining his feet he sprang to one of the open doors and looking out saw nobody. Then he ran to the other, with the same result. He was evidently alone on some sort of a boat, which at that moment was drifting beneath a great iron bridge.

CHAPTER XI.

UNCLE PHIN'S DANGER.

FOR a moment poor Arthur, who knew nothing of boats and had never been on one before unless it was a New York ferry-boat, stood irresolute and frightened, without the slightest idea of what had happened or what he ought to do. The cry that he heard had not sounded a bit like Uncle Phin's voice, and if it was his what had become of him? He was not on the boat, nor, so far as Arthur could discover, was he in the water. Upon seeing the bridge overhead the boy readily comprehended that the shock which had flung him to the floor was caused by the boat drifting against one of its great stone piers; but this did not explain Uncle Phin's disappearance.

In his fear and distress of mind he began to call wildly: "Uncle Phin! Oh, dear Uncle Phin! where are you?"

"Hyar I is, Honey," came a feeble voice from the other end of the boat, and Arthur sprang joyfully in that direction.

As the boat had swung around on striking the bridge pier, its after end now pointed down stream, and Arthur had been standing at the bow, gazing back on the place where he was afraid Uncle Phin had been left. Now, as he reached the other end of the boat, he saw the old man's white head and black face, just on the surface of the water, but a short distance from where he stood. He seemed to be sitting astride of some object, to which he clung desperately. Every now and then it would sink, and poor Uncle Phin would disappear completely, only to re-appear a moment later, spluttering, choking, and exhibiting every sign of the utmost terror.

For a moment Arthur did not in the least comprehend the situation, and could not imagine what it was to which Uncle Phin was clinging. When it suddenly occurred to him that it was the long steering sweep, the other end of which projected above his head over the roof of the cabin, his first impulse, and the one on which he acted, was to spring to this inboard end and throw his weight upon it, with the idea of lifting the old negro clear of the water. As the steering sweep was a very nicely balanced see-saw, and as Uncle Phin's body in the water, weighed less than Arthur's out of it, the boy's effort was crowned with a complete success, though its result was not exactly what he had anticipated.

To be sure, as Arthur flung himself upon one end of the long pole, the old man, astride the bit of plank fastened to its other end, was lifted into the air. It was, however, so suddenly and unexpectedly, that he lost his balance, toppled over, and again disappeared headforemost beneath the water. At the same time the boy, at the inner end of the seesaw, was bumped down on the cabin roof. Then Uncle Phin's end again descended into the water, just in time for the old man to grasp it as he came to the surface.

With great difficulty he struggled into his former position, and turning a reproachful gaze on Arthur said:

"Don't you do it again, Honey. I 'se no doubt you means all right; but anodder fling like dat ar, would drown de old man shuah."

"I did n't mean to, Uncle Phin! Indeed, I

did n't!" cried poor Arthur, in great distress. "I only meant to try and help you and lift you from the water."

"Well, you done it, Honey, shuah 'nuff; but I would n' try no more sich 'speriments. If you 'll frow me de end ob de rope, what 's lying jes inside the do, and tie de odder end to dat ar pos, I reckin I kin pull myself up outen de water."

Arthur quickly did as directed, and in a few minutes more had the satisfaction of seeing his dear old friend rescued from his perilous position, and seated safely on the deck. As the water-soaked man sat there, recovering from his exhaustion, and grateful for the warmth of the hot morning sun, he shook his head, and said:

"I allus heerd tell dat salorin was a resky bizness, an dat dem what goes down into de sea in ships sees wonerful tings; but I nebber spected ole Phin Dale ebber sperience it all fer his own sef."

After his strength was somewhat restored, Uncle Phin instructed Arthur to keep a sharp lookout for any more bridges, and went into the cabin to light a fire and prepare breakfast. A good supply of dry wood and a box of matches having been provided, he quickly had a cheerful blaze crackling on his rude hearth. While it was burning down to a bed of red coals, he mixed the meal, salt, and water, that he intended should be transformed into a corn-pone, set the coffee water on to boil, and cut two slices of bacon. The smoke of the fire found its way out of the cabin through a square hatch that Brace Barlow had cut in the roof directly above it.

In less than an hour the bed of coals had done its duty. The corn-pone had been baked on a flat stone, previously rubbed with a bacon rind, and set up at a sharp angle in the hottest corner of the fireplace. The slices of bacon were done to a turn, and four fresh eggs had been fried with them. The coffee was hot and strong, and there was maple sugar to sweeten it. Taken altogether, it was a breakfast that would have pleased a much more fastidious person than hungry little Arthur Dale Dustin, and he enjoyed it as, it seemed to him, he never had enjoyed a meal before.

Uncle Phin's delight at seeing his "lil Marse" eat so heartily was unbounded, and they both found so much pleasure in their novel housekeeping that the mishap of an hour before was forgotten, and they would willingly have agreed to drift along in this happy way for the rest of their lives.

After every scrap of food had been eaten, and only grounds remained in the coffee-pot, Uncle Phin began to clear the table, which was an empty packing-box, shake the table-cloth, which was a newspaper, and wash the dishes; while Arthur set to work to tidy up the cabin. He made the beds, which only took about one minute each, placed his precious book carefully on one of the shelves, and then looked about for a broom with which to sweep the floor. There was none.

"Why, Uncle Phin!" exclaimed the boy, "if we have n't come off and forgotten the broom!"

"So we has, Honey! so we has!" replied the old man, pausing in his work and assuming an expression of mock dismay, "I ricollec now, when de furnichure man putten in dem elergent brack walnut bedstids, he say, 'Misto Phin Dale, don you fergit somefin'; and I say, 'No, Misto Furnichure man, I reckin not.' Now, he mus er been meanin de broom all de time, an hyar we is come off an lef it behin."

"You are making fun of me, you know you are," laughed Arthur: "but really, I do need a broom very much, for I can't make this place look tidy without one."

"You mus hab one, ob cose," said Uncle Phin, "an we'll jes run inter de sho and fin some white birch trees, an Unc Phin make you a twig broom, jes de fines you ebber seen."

They were both glad of an excuse to stop and make a landing, for they were enjoying their voyage so much that they feared it might come to an end more quickly than they wished it to. So they went on deck, and watched for a good opportunity to run ashore.

At last they drifted close into a grassy bank, above which were a number of huge oil-tanks, a brick building, and a neat white cottage. It was a pumping station on one of the great pipe lines through which crude petroleum is conveyed from the wells of the oil region to the distant seaboard refineries. At that time it was thought necessary to have relay stations of tanks, and pumps to force the oil along from one to another, every five or six miles. Of late years, however, the pumps have grown larger and stronger, until, on a recently constructed pipe-line leading into Chicago, one immense pumping engine forces the oil along the entire distance of 250 miles.

As the Ark drifted slowly along in front of this pleasant-looking place, Uncle Phin, directing Arthur how to steer, loosened the side sweep that was farthest from shore, and, by rowing with it, headed their craft in toward the bank. In a minute more she was so close to it that Arthur could easily spring to the narrow beach, carrying with him the end of a rope, that he made fast to a tree.

CHAPTER XII.

A TORRENT OF FLAME.

WHEN the boat was properly secured, Uncle Phin, leaving Arthur to look out for it, shouldered his axe and went in search of a birch tree. Within half an hour he returned, bringing a great bundle of twigs and the interesting information that there was a little boy and a little girl up in the bushes picking blackberries.

"Oh, can't I go up there and pick some too?" asked Arthur; "they would be so good for dinner, and if I got enough you might make a pie, you know." He was fully in earnest, for he had such firm faith in Uncle Phin's culinary skill that he believed he could make anything good to eat that anybody else could.

The old man only laughed at this, but said he might go if he wanted to; and the boy, taking a tin-cup in which to hold the berries, ran off, happily enough, to find the children. When he discovered them they were both standing still, bashfully looking at him, the little girl, in a pink sun-bonnet that reminded him of Cynthia's, half hidden behind her brother and evidently just ready to run away.

The new-comer at once opened conversation by saying: "How do you do? I am very glad to see you, because I have n't very many friends. My name is Arthur Dale Dustin. What is yours?"

The boy said his was Bert and his sister's was Sue, and that their other name was Chapman. He added that their father was engineer of the pumping station, and that nobody else lived anywhere near there.

Within five minutes they were thoroughly well acquainted, and were all busily picking the luscious berries that abounded in that vicinity. Arthur said it reminded him of a fairy story, and little Sue Chapman said she loved fairy tales, only she had not heard very many. So Arthur began to tell them the story of the "Mermaid," which was one that he had read to Cynthia; but he could not remember it very well, and said if they would go down with him to where he lived he would read it to them out of his book.

They readily agreed to this, and were so delighted with the queer house-boat and all that they saw on it that it was some time before they were ready to listen to the story of the mermaid. When it was finished they said they must go home now, but invited Arthur to come up to the house and see them after dinner.

That afternoon he met Mr. Chapman and Mrs. Chapman, and saw the great pumping engine at work, and was allowed to climb up and look into one of the large tanks that held thousands of barrels of oil, and had altogether a most interesting and happy time. The best of all though was playing with the dogs, of which there were three, a mother and two half-grown pups, all thoroughbred bull terriers.

The boy enjoyed these so much, and was so fascinated with their playfulness and intelligence, and Mr. Chapman took such a fancy to him, that he told Bert and Sue they might make their new friend a present of one of the pups if they wished.

As Arthur had never owned a real live pet in his life, this seemed a most generous offer and he thanked the Chapmans warmly. They gave him his choice of the two pups, and each showed so many good points that it was a long time before he could make up his mind which to take. At length he chose one that was brindled, and had a white tip to his tail. His name was "Russet," but as the young Chapmans called him "Rusty," Arthur decided that he would call him so too.

He carried the pup in his arms down to the boat; but all the way it cried piteously at being taken from its home, and struggled hard to get free. Arthur made a bed for it at the foot of his own bunk and tried to feed it, but the pup refused to accept his kindness, and only cried and whined and begged to be let out at one of the closed doors. Finally even good-natured Uncle Phin lost his patience and said the pup needed a good whipping to make him keep quiet.

"Oh, no, indeed, Uncle Phin!" exclaimed Arthur, reproachfully; "I would n't whip him for anything. How would you like to be whipped because you cried at being taken away from your mamma? I've made up my mind that I won't make him unhappy any longer; and so, though I should love dearly to keep him if he wanted to stay, I shall just carry him back to his home."

True to this resolve, the tender-hearted little fellow did carry poor "Rusty" back up the hill, and was made even happier by witnessing the extravagant joy of the pup and the mother dog at once more seeing each other, than he had been by receiving the Chapmans' gift.

They made him stay to supper, after which the whole family said they would escort him down to the boat, of which Bert and Sue had talked so much, that their parents were curious to see it. So, taking a lantern with them, for it was growing dark, they started down the slope, at the bottom of which they met Uncle Phin, just coming to look for his "lil Marse," at whose long absence he had grown anxious.

Mr. Chapman, who was much interested in this voyage of the old negro and his young master, had brought down a small lamp and a gallon of oil for it, as a present to them; for Arthur had told him that they had no light on board. Mrs. Chapman brought a loaf of bread. Bert brought half a dozen eggs laid by his own hen, and little Sue, who could think of nothing else, brought a bunch of flowers from her own garden. They had a very merry time over the presentation of these gifts, for each of which Uncle Phin returned thanks in his own funny, earnest way.

When Arthur said he wished he had something to give in return for them to remember him by, Mrs. Chapman said that if he would only read to them one of the stories out of his fairy book that the children had told her of, it would be one of the most acceptable presents he could make them. This the boy was willing enough to do, and when the new lamp was lighted and placed on the packing-box that served as a table, and they had all found seats, he read to them the story of "Little Klaus" who made bushels of money by everything that he undertook.

When he finished they all thanked him, and Bert said if he had a bushel of money he would buy a pony. Little Sue said she would get a great big doll, as big as a live baby, that could talk; and her mother said if they only had money enough, they would live near a town where they could have neighbors, and where the children could go to school. Mr. Chapman said it would be very nice to have a bushel of money and a fine house, but that they should be very thankful for the one they had, especially when such a storm was coming up, as was about to burst over them at that moment.

Sure enough it was thundering, and the guests of the evening had not been gone from the Ark many minutes before great drops of rain began to fall. Nearer and nearer swept the storm, and blacker and blacker grew the night, until the awful glare of the lightning was almost continuous, and the crash of the thunder was deafening. Silently, hand in hand, the two occupants of the house-boat sat and watched it.

Suddenly there fell a blinding, dazzling ball of fire, accompanied by such an awful burst of thunder as shook the solid earth. The next instant the whole sky was lighted by a vast column of flame that seemed to spring from the hillside directly above the place where the Ark lay moored. One of the great oil tanks had been struck by the lightning, and now a raging, roaring mass of flame shot up fifty feet into the air above it, lighting the river and the whole storm-swept country for miles around with its fierce, lurid glare. It was a grand but fearful sight, and the boy clung closer to the old man, as he gazed upon it with an eager fascination.

They could not at first understand the deep booming sounds that they began to hear above the roar of the storm, soon after the fire broke out, and which were repeated at regular intervals of a few minutes each. Then Arthur remembered what Brace Barlow had told him about firing cannon-balls into burning oil-tanks, that the oil might run out through the holes thus made, and the danger of an explosion be lessened. Mr. Chapman was shooting at this tank with a small cannon that he kept on hand for just such an emergency.

All at once the contents of the tank seemed to boil over. A fountain of blazing oil burst from it and poured down its sides, the oil running from the shot-holes near its base took fire, and in another instant a fierce torrent of flame came rushing down the slope, directly toward the little house-boat moored at its foot.

Poor Uncle Phin dropped on his knees in an agony of fear, crying: "O Lawd! O de good Lawd, hab mussy on us, an deliber us frum de fiery funness"; while to Arthur it seemed as though they were in most imminent peril.

CHAPTER XIII.

HOW THE ARK WAS SAVED.

IF the wind had been blowing from across the river, so as to hold the Ark close to the bank against which she was moored, nothing could have saved her from destruction by the torrent of blazing oil that rushed down the slope. Even her occupants would have stood but a slight chance of escaping. The stream of leaping flame was so wide, and came toward them with such extraordinary swiftness, that, before they could have reached the shore and run beyond its limits in either direction, it would have been upon them. Their only chance would have been to throw themselves into the swift current of the river from the opposite side of their boat, with the hope of gaining the bank at a safe distance below.

Uncle Phin was helpless with terror and completely bewildered by the suddenness of the peril that threatened them. Thus it was entirely owing to Arthur's presence of mind and quick wit, that their boat was saved and they escaped the necessity of taking the desperate plunge that would probably have drowned one or both of them. The boy had noticed that the storm came from over the hills on their side of the river, and how, as the fierce blasts swept down and struck the broadside of the Ark, she tugged and strained at her moorings. Now he remembered this, and was quick to turn his observations to account.

Seizing the axe he severed at a single blow the rope holding the boat at one end, and then, running to the other, cut that with equal promptness. Next, thrusting a long pole into Uncle Phin's trembling hands, he bade the old man shove off from shore with all his might, at one end, while, with a lighter pole, he did the same thing at the other. Their feeble strength would have availed little but for the powerful aid lent by the favoring gale. While this hurled the advancing flames fiercely toward them, it also drove them, at first slowly, then more rapidly, beyond reach of the danger.

There were hardly ten feet of open water between

the Ark and the shore she had just left when the flames sprang down the bank and began to spread over the surface of the river, the oil burning here as readily as on land. For a minute it seemed as though the fire must catch and devour them after all. Its flames leaped eagerly forward, like a million writhing serpents, with red-forked tongues, darting after their prey.

"Push, Uncle Phin! Push for your life!" shouted Arthur from his end of the boat, where he was breathlessly exerting every ounce of strength that his sturdy young frame could yield.

"I 'se a pushin, Honey!" answered the old man, with the veins of his forehead standing out like whipcords. "I is a pushin; but onless de good Lawd pushin wif us, we hain't got no show."

But the good Lord did push with these, his helpless ones, and his strong wind bore their drifting boat forward faster than it did the hungry flames. The current, of course, set them down stream at the same time, and thus, moving in a diagonal direction, they soon found themselves in safety. They were beyond the limits of the sea of fire, that extended for a mile down the river, and a quarter of that distance out toward its centre. Then the old man and the boy laid down their now useless poles and watched the wonderfully beautiful but fearful sight, while they recovered their spent breath.

The great tank was still vomiting forth sheets of flame and clouds of smoke. None of the others had caught fire, and an occasional gleam of light, reflected from the white walls of the Chapmans' cottage, showed them that it was still safe.

At length, as they were rapidly nearing the opposite side of the river, the current bore them around a sharp turn that almost instantly hid the whole glowing scene from them, and plunged them into a darkness, the more intense on account of the recent glare.

With this turn of the river the gale, now acting on the other side of the boat, drove it back toward the bank they had left, and thus, for several hours, as they followed the windings of the crooked stream, they were carried now almost to one side and then nearly to the other. As they could see absolutely nothing of where they were, or whither they were going, they were quite ignorant of their surroundings. Nor did they know what happened when, about midnight, their boat was driven violently upon some obstruction, and its movement was suddenly arrested.

The storm had passed so that there was no longer any lightning to give instantaneous photographs of the scene about them. The wind still blew a gale; and, as they could hear it lashing the branches of the forest trees, apparently directly above their heads, they concluded that they must have been driven ashore.

Although both Arthur and Uncle Phin were too excited, and too anxious, to go to bed, there was nothing they could do to improve their situation until the morning light should disclose its features. So they closed the doors and windows of their house and lighted the new lamp. How snug and cheerful the rude little cabin now looked. How home-like it seemed, and what a fine shelter it was from the gale that was howling outside.

Arthur said he was hungry; and, as Uncle Phin said he was hungry also, they drew upon their slender store of provisions for a light lunch, after which Arthur read aloud from his book the tale of "The Steadfast Lead Soldier." The old negro thought it a very nice story, though not so good as it would be had the lead soldier been alive. Then he told Arthur, for about the thousandth time, the story of how Brer Rabbit and Brer Fox went a-fishing, and before it was finished the tired child was fast asleep. Then Uncle Phin lifted him gently into his bunk, and finding that the gale had subsided, almost to a calm, concluded to go to bed himself.

So the Ark was again left to take care of itself, and when its inmates next awoke it was not only broad daylight, but nearly noon. They now discovered that their craft had indeed been driven ashore, on the same side of the river that they had left the preceding evening, though, of course, several miles below the pumping station. There were now no houses in sight, nor any traces of human beings, nothing so far as they could see but a thick forest. After a few ineffectual efforts they found that it was useless to try and push the Ark off with poles into deep water. She was hard and fast aground, and they could not budge her a single inch.

So they decided to have breakfast first and make up their minds what to do afterwards, and while Uncle Phin prepared the simple meal, Arthur made the beds and swept out the cabin with his fine new broom of birch twigs.

After breakfast, or rather after dinner; for, although they did not know it, it was past one o'clock before they finished their meal, the entire crew of the Ark got overboard to examine her situation. They found she had grounded on a sand-bar that afforded her an easy resting-place, but which also held her in a firm grasp. Uncle Phin cut down a young tree, trimmed off its branches, and, using it as a lever, with a large rock as a fulcrum, tried to pry the boat off the bar, but to no purpose. The combined strength of the old man and the boy produced not the slightest effect upon her, and no wonder, for all the strength they could command was but weakness, compared with what was needed.

It was a very unfortunate situation, particularly as they had only provisions enough to last a few days, and knew not where they were to obtain more. Then, too, as it was now the month of October, no more high water could be expected that year, and, in the meantime, the river would be apt to fall lower and lower, leaving their boat high and dry.

In going ashore to cut his lever, Uncle Phin had discovered a road, running parallel with the river. Now he proposed to walk down this road until he came to a house, in the hope of obtaining help, provided Arthur was not afraid to remain alone and look after the Ark.

Of course Arthur was not afraid, he scorned the idea. What should he be afraid of? It was not likely that anybody would hurt a little boy like him. So Uncle Phin left him, and, wading ashore, disappeared down the forest road.

For some time the boy amused himself about the boat; but his resources were few, and after an hour or so, he grew lonely, and began to watch anxiously for Uncle Phin's return. Exposed to the full glare of the afternoon sun, the boat became as hot as an oven; and finally Arthur decided to take his book and wade ashore. There he would find a comfortable place, in the cool shade of the trees, from which he might the sooner perceive anybody approaching along the road.

He found just such a place as he had longed for; a deliciously cool, shady glade, surrounded by spreading oak trees, and commanding a limited view of the road. After sitting here for some time, he discovered that there were ripe berries on the opposite side of the glade. When he had gathered and eaten these, he saw more berries beyond them, and still more at a greater distance. Then he found some lovely flowers, and thought it would be a fine idea to gather enough of them to decorate the cabin of the Ark against Uncle Phin's return. So he strolled carelessly on, from berries to flowers, and from one flower to another, until, all at once, the deepening shadows roused him to a knowledge of the fact that the sun was setting, and that he could no longer see either the road or the river.

CHAPTER XIV.

A CAMP OF TRAMPS.

IT was evidently high time to be getting home, and the boy started back in the direction he had just come. He was certain that it was the right direction, and yet the trees and bushes kept getting thicker and thicker, and he missed the open glades through which he had been strolling. This was clearly the wrong track; and, facing directly about, he now attempted to retrace his latest course.

It was rapidly growing dark; strange night sounds were beginning to be heard in the forest, and a great dread began to clutch at the boy's heart. Was he really lost, as the Babes in the Wood had been, and would he die there, and be covered with leaves, so that even his body could not be found, and nobody would ever know what had become of him?

He began to call aloud; but only the forest echoes mocked him, and the night birds answered him with harsh cries. At length it was too dark to even try and walk any farther. The little fellow, frightened and weary, sank down at the foot of a great tree, that seemed to lean over him with an air of protection and sympathy.

He would not cry. Uncle Phin had said that none of the Dales ever cried after they were grown up, and he was a Dale, almost grown up. Two or three big tears rolled silently down his cheeks; but then that was something that might happen to almost anybody, at any time. It could not be counted as crying.

As he sat there in the darkness, trying to be brave because he was a Dale, the sound of a peculiar, long-drawn, far-away cry, caused him involuntarily to look around; though, of course, he did not expect to see anything through the darkness. He did see something, though, and it was a light. It was not a bright, clear light; but a dim glow, just visible between the tree trunks, and evidently at quite a distance from where he sat.

The boy's spirits rose with a bound. He dashed

away the stealthy tear drops, and sprang to his feet. Things were coming out all right after all; for a light meant people, who, according to simple-hearted little Arthur's experience of the world, would be kind to him. They would probably invite him to stay to supper, and show him the way to the Ark afterwards. Then he would ask them to help him and Uncle Phin get the boat afloat, and his becoming lost would turn out to be the very best kind of a thing that could have happened after all.

While these thoughts passed through his mind, the boy was making his way, as rapidly as possible, through the woods in the direction of the light, that grew brighter and more distinct with each step. He still carried his precious book in one hand, and the great bunch of flowers that he had gathered, in the other. Suddenly he came to an abrupt pause on the edge of a shallow ravine, through which laughed and tumbled a small brook. The sides of the ravine were quite steep, and, almost at his feet, the boy saw a sight that filled him with amazement.

About a glowing fire, occupying all sorts of easy positions, were grouped a number of men and one boy. They were ragged, dirty, and unshaven.

Their clothes were made up of odds and ends. Some of them were smoking short black pipes; some were talking loudly; and others lay perfectly still, as though asleep. Two of the number seemed to be preparing supper; for they were at work about the fire, and were evidently anxious regarding the contents of some tin cans, and several battered kettles. At a short distance from the fire were two or three rude huts of poles and branches.

Although Arthur did not know it at the time, this was a tramps' camp, to which all these vagrants of society, who happened to be prowling about that part of the country, flocked when night overtook them. Sometimes one or more, who were tired of tramping, and who had begged or stolen a stock of provisions, would remain here for several days, so that, from early spring until quite late in the autumn, the camp was never without a greater or less number of occupants.

Now, although Arthur had never had any practical experience with tramps, except to gaze curiously, from a respectful distance, at the few specimens he had seen, he instinctively shrank from making his presence known to the rough-looking fellows gathered beneath him. It was pleasant to see the cheerful firelight, to hear the sound of voices, and to know that there were other human beings besides himself in that dark forest. It would also be very pleasant to the hungry boy if he could have some supper. Still, to venture down among those men might prove very unpleasant. So Arthur wisely decided to bear his hunger as best he might, and study them from a safe distance, at least for a while longer.

All at once, from some part of the camp beyond the circle of firelight, came the same melancholy long-drawn cry that had first directed the boy's attention to this place, and he now recognized it as the howl of a dog in distress.

At the sound, the largest and most powerful of all the tramps, who had been lying motionless stretched at full length on the ground, sprang up, and in a fierce voice exclaimed:

"You Kid, fetch that pup here! we'll see if we can't give him something to ki-yi for, or else we'll stop his infernal yelp entirely."

The one boy of the camp, who answered to the name of "Kid," and was a tough-looking young rascal, larger and apparently a year or two older than Arthur, hastened to obey this command. He disappeared, and in a minute returned dragging after him, by means of a bit of rope about its neck that was evidently choking it, a dog. As the bright firelight fell full upon the animal, Arthur was amazed to recognize it as the very one that had been presented to him by the Chapmans the day before. There could be no doubt of it; for there were the same erect sharp-pointed ears, the same white-tipped little tail, and the same brindled markings. It was indeed poor Rusty; and Arthur's heart ached to see him in so wretched a plight. How could he have come there? What were they about to do with him? This last question was quickly answered.

The big tramp took the rope from the lad's hand, at the same time bidding him go and cut a hickory switch. "See that it's a good one too," he added.

This command was obeyed as the other had been, and in a few minutes the switch was ready.

"Now whale him while I hold him," ordered the big tramp, savagely. "We'll give him a chance to do all his howling at once, and then we'll have some peace for the rest of the night. Lay it on solid, and if you kill him, so much the better."

Arthur's blood boiled at these words. How could anybody be so cruel? Would the boy dare beat *his* dog?

The heavy switch was uplifted and brought down with vicious force on the animal's back. The dog uttered a sharp cry of pain and terror.

Again was the switch lifted; but before it could descend it was snatched from the boy's hand and flung away; while he was confronted by a sturdy young figure with blazing eyes. "How dare you strike my dog?" cried Arthur, in a voice that choked and trembled with anger. "He is mine! My very own! And I won't have him hurt. I won't, I say."

The other boy stared at this one in open-mouthed amazement, while the tramps, who had been startled by the sight of the strange little figure, as it dashed into their camp from the dark forest, now gathered about the two to see the fun.

"Well, my bantam," said the big tramp to Arthur, "I don't know who you are, nor where you come from; but you talk pretty big about *your* dog. Kid here says it's his dog, and I reckon you'll have to settle it between you. Can you fight?"

"I don't want to fight," replied Arthur, looking the big tramp bravely in the face.

"Oh, well then, it's the Kid's dog, and he'll do as he pleases with him. Kid, give the cur a kick."

The boy lifted his foot but again Arthur sprang in front of him. "You sha'n't kick him, even if I have to fight you to make you stop it!" he cried. Then he clenched his fists, and his face grew very pale.

"That's right, sonny!" said the big tramp, approvingly. "I'll back you and hold your picture-book and nosegay. Take off your jacket like a little man. Now, fellers, form a ring and give the bantams a fair show."

CHAPTER XV.

ARTHUR'S FIGHT TO SAVE RUSTY.

IN all his life Arthur had never before found it necessary to fight, though he had certainly received provocation enough from his Cousin Dick to do so more than once. His own father had taught him to hate fighting and to avoid it if possible, as he would anything else that was ungentlemanly and wrong. At the same time Mr. Dustin had been too wise a man not to know that occasions may arise in everybody's life when it becomes absolutely necessary to fight. He believed, for instance, that it is right and proper to do so in defence of the weak and helpless who have claims upon us for protection, provided that is the only way of defending them, and this principle he had thoroughly instilled into his child's mind.

Mr. Dustin also believed that every boy should be taught to use the weapons with which nature has provided him—namely, his fists—for the protection of himself and others, just as he should be taught to read and write or do a thousand other things necessary to his success and happiness in life.

Thus believing, and having been himself one of the best boxers in his college gymnasium, he had begun to instruct his little son in the art of self-defence on the very day that the boy's mother began to teach him his letters. Now, therefore, although Arthur had never fought a battle with any other boy, he had a very fair knowledge of what he ought to do under the circumstances, and of how to do it.

All his father's talks upon the subject flashed into his mind, and he seemed to remember every word of them. He could almost hear the dear voice say: "Never fight if you can help it, but if the time comes that you feel it to be your duty, then pitch in with all your heart, with all your strength, and with all your skill. Then fight just as long as you can stand, or until you have won a victory."

In the present instance, surrounded as he was by fierce-looking, hard-hearted men, who acknowledged no law but that of brute force, and with poor little Rusty crouching at his feet, so certain was the boy of his duty, that he prepared for the coming struggle with a brave heart, though with a very white face.

The boy called "Kid" was perfectly willing to fight; in fact, there was nothing he enjoyed more, especially when, as in this case, he saw the prospect of an easy victory before him. So, as he stood up in front of Arthur, the firelight disclosed a broad grin on his dirty face. He looked so much stronger and heavier than his antagonist, that some of the men were touched with pity for the little fellow, and murmured that it was n't a square deal.

"That's all right," said the big tramp, who had taken charge of the affair. "The young chap's got sand or else he would n't be here. He's been talking pretty big too, and now he's got the chance to show whether he can back up his words or not."

To the amazement of the spectators the battle was a long and a hard one; for the new-comer's pluck and skill were evenly matched against the other's weight and a dogged pride that forbade him to yield to one younger and smaller than himself. Still, he was in the wrong, and he knew it; while Arthur was in the right, and knew that he was. The boy who was fighting in defence of the weak and the helpless never once thought of giving in, and so the other had to. They finally went to the ground together, with Arthur on top, and this ended the struggle. The "Kid" began to cry: "Lemme up! lemme up! I don't want to fight no more wid a perfessional. Lemme up!"

Then Arthur left him, and walked to where poor little Rusty was crouching, with his rope held by one of the tramps. Taking the rope in his hand, and lifting his brave, flushed face, blood-stained from a slight cut on his forehead, to that of the big tramp who had ordered the pup to be beaten, the boy asked: "Is he my dog now?"

"Of course he is, sonny; of course he is!" answered the big man, promptly. "You've fought the bulliest kind of a fight for him, and I'd like to see the man as would try to take him from you."

As he spoke, the big tramp glared about him, as though wishing somebody would dare dispute his words, but nobody did. Every one of those who now crowded about the boy, anxious to shake hands with him and congratulate him on his victory, expressed the heartiest approval of what the big man said. They all seemed to regard Arthur as a hero, and to feel highly honored by his presence in their camp. Even *his* dog received a full share of praise and petting, and was utterly bewildered by the sudden turn in the tide of popular opinion concerning him.

Seeing that the young champion was rendered uncomfortable by the over-officiousness of those who crowded about him, the big tramp, who seemed to exercise an acknowledged authority over them, ordered the rest to clear out, and leave the little chap to him. Then he took Arthur to the brook, and bathed his face and hands, and even his bare feet, in its cool waters, with a degree of tenderness surprising in one so big and rough.

A few minutes later supper was announced, and the big tramp made Arthur sit beside him on the ground, in front of a kettle that contained a most delicious-smelling stew of chicken and potatoes and onions and green corn, and several other things. To be sure, Arthur was obliged to eat his portion out of a hastily improvised bowl of birch bark, made for him by his big friend, with a rude wooden spoon provided by the same ingenious individual;

but how good it was! How often that bark bowl was refilled, and how proud the cooks were to have the hero of the feast thus compliment them so highly.

As for little Rusty, who seemed to recognize Arthur as his friend and protector, and kept close beside him, there never was a dog treated with greater consideration. Everybody wanted to feed him, and kept tossing choice morsels of food to him. He ate everything thus offered, with perfect impartiality, until at length he had no room for another morsel, and even the daintiest bits of chicken failed to tempt him.

After supper all the tramps were anxious to learn something of Arthur's history, and who had taught him to fight so skilfully, and how he happened to visit their camp. So he told them about his own dear father, who had given him boxing lessons, and about living with Uncle John and Aunt Nancy, and how he and Uncle Phin had decided to go to his grandfather's in Virginia, and were travelling in a boat, and how it had run aground so that they could n't get it off, and Uncle Phin had gone in search of help, and how he happened to get lost in the woods, and finally how he discovered their camp; all of which was listened to with absorbing interest.

When he finished, the big tramp spoke up and said: "Well, fellers, from this little chap's account of hisself, I don't see but what him and his old Uncle Phin is travelling through the country pretty much the same as we does, like gentlemen of leisure and independent means, as it were. In fact I should call 'em a couple of honest tramps, as is making their way through the world without asking no odds of nobody."

"That's so," assented several voices.

"Such being the case," continued the big man, "It is clearly our dooty to help 'em out of the fix they've got into, and I move that we all go down to the river, first thing in the morning, and set their old scow afloat."

As this motion seemed to meet with general approval, Arthur was cordially invited to spend the night in the tramps' camp, and was assured that they would guide him to the Ark, and that it should be started on its voyage the very first thing in the morning. As there really seemed nothing else for him to do, the little fellow accepted the invitation, though he wished he could get back to the boat that night, and thus relieve the anxiety that he knew Uncle Phin must be suffering on account of his unexplained disappearance.

In the meantime he had recovered his book from the big tramp, who had held it during the fight, and it now lay on the grass beside him. He had mentioned that he sometimes read stories from this book to Uncle Phin, and now the big tramp said to him: "Look here, sonny, why won't you read a story to us out of your book, just to pass away the time? If you will, I will give you some information that may prove useful to you in your travels, but which you can't find in any book in the world."

CHAPTER XVI.

THE MEANING OF SOME QUEER SIGNS.

ARTHUR said he would gladly read to the tramps if they cared to hear him, and at the same time he wondered what valuable information the man could possibly give him.

Then all the tramps gathered as near to him as they could, and Arthur, sitting where the firelight shone brightest, with one hand laid protectingly on little Rusty, opened his precious book, and read the first story he came to, which happened to be that of " The Ugly Duckling."

It was a striking picture, that of the fair-haired child, sitting in the red glow of the firelight, and reading a fairy tale to the rough men crowded about him, their uncouth figures half disclosed and half hidden in the dusky shadows. Close behind the big tramp, who was his father, sat the boy with whom Arthur had fought, still looking sullen and crestfallen over his recent defeat, and occasionally casting glances of mingled envy and hate at his rival.

As the tale proceeded, his hard, young face took on a softer expression, and when it was finished he heaved a great sigh.

"Well, Kid," said the big tramp, turning to him at the conclusion of the story, "what do you think of that for a yarn? You are a pretty ugly sort of a duck yourself, and who knows but what you may turn out to be a swan after all, some of these fine days."

"It'll be a goose more like," muttered one of the men; and Arthur, looking pityingly at the lad, wondered which it would be.

Now it was the big tramp's turn to fulfil his part of the bargain. This he began to do by taking a bit of chalk from his pocket and drawing with it several rude figures like these, $\times \times \Phi - \sqrt{}$ on a piece of birch bark. Showing them to Arthur, he told him that these were signs understood by all the tramps of the country, and that whenever they saw them chalked on gate-posts or fences or other conspicuous places near houses, they knew at once what they meant. "This, for instance," he said, pointing to one of the signs, "means 'Stingy people in this house; won't give a poor tramp anything.' This one means, 'Savage dog in here'; and this, 'Good people, and plenty to eat.'" Another meant, "Man here keeps a gun for tramps"; and still another, "Only women folks here; no danger." He also said that the older and best-known tramps had their private marks or autographs, which were very generally known and recognized by all the others along their particular lines of travel.

Arthur was greatly interested in this, and made copies of several of the marks thus shown him, so as to impress them upon his memory, though at that time he could not foresee that they would ever be of any use. At the close of this novel lesson, the big tramp told him that his name was Sandy Grimes, and showed him his own private mark or autograph, which was M, and said that Arthur was at liberty to use it, in proof of their friendship, whenever he found himself in company with any other tramps.

The boy thanked him politely for this favor, though thinking to himself that he hoped the time would never come when he should care to claim such a friendship. Then Arthur said he was tired, and would like to go to sleep, whereupon Sandy Grimes showed him a bed of dry leaves beside a big log near enough to the fire to feel its warmth, and told him he could lie down there. So there the tired little fellow lay, with Rusty nestled close beside him, and watched the stars twinkling overhead until he fell asleep.

Although on this occasion Arthur breathed great quantities of the night air that his Aunt Nancy had declared to be poison, its injurious effects were not apparent when he awoke the next morning, looking as bright and fresh as though he had slept in the downiest of beds. To be sure he felt somewhat stiff and sore; but after his encounter with the young tramp, it would have been most surprising if he had not.

The sun was just rising as he made his way to the brook to dip his face in its cool waters; but the camp was already astir. Tramps are proverbially lazy, but they are always among the earliest of risers. From the cheap lodging-houses and police-stations of the city they are turned out at daylight. The same thing happens in the country, where the thrifty farmer routs them out from his barn or haystacks, and hunger drives them from their camps at the same early hour. A want of food was what set this particular camp astir by sunrise on this occasion; for its occupants had exhausted their entire supply on the feast of the previous evening. Now they were setting forth to beg, or steal, something to eat at the nearest farm-houses and villages.

Some of them, careless of their promise made the night before to go with Arthur and help him and Uncle Phin get their boat afloat, had already left, while others sullenly refused to keep their word, now that they were reminded of it. However, five of them, including the big tramp and his boy, said they were going that way anyhow, and did n't mind giving the youngster a lift with his scow if it did n't take too long and prove too hard work. So, in a few minutes after leaving his bed by the old log, Arthur found himself walking down the ravine toward the river in company with five as disreputable and rascally-looking tramps as could be found in the country.

He had not forgotten poor little Rusty. Oh, no

indeed! Nor had the dog forgotten him, but now followed close at his heels without paying the slightest attention to any other person in the party. He had been stolen by the "Kid" from the Chapmans' house during the excitement caused by the burning oil tank, and had evidently suffered much at the hands of his captor, for never after that day did he see a tramp without growling and showing his teeth at him.

The tramps' camp was located but a few hundred yards from the road that ran along the river bank, and the relief party had hardly turned into it before Arthur, with a cry of joy, sprang forward and flung himself into the arms of Uncle Phin, who, looking the picture of misery and utter dejection, was hobbling toward them.

The old man was so overcome by joy and bewilderment that for a few moments he was utterly speechless. Then he broke out with "Tank de good Lawd, Honey, I is foun you! Ole Phin die ob de heart broke shuah if he did n't fin you pretty quick, an he's bin sarchin fo you all de night long." This was said with such a heartfelt earnestness, that the boy realized in a moment how greatly his old friend had suffered.

Although Uncle Phin had found several houses during his absence of the afternoon before, none of their inmates had been willing to return and help him get the Ark afloat. He had not got back to it until after sunset, and then, to his dismay, had found it dark and deserted.

Too greatly distressed to eat or sleep, he had spent the night in wandering up and down the road hunting, and calling for, his "lil Marse," and now that he had found him, his joy was almost too great for expression.

It was but a short distance to where the Ark lay aground, and it was but a five minutes' job for those sturdy tramps to work her off the sand-bar and set her once more afloat.

The last thing Arthur did before scrambling aboard was to shake hands with the boy whom he had fought the evening before, and, as he bade him good-bye, he said : " I hope you won't be an 'ugly duckling' much longer."

Then, with its three passengers safely aboard, the Ark slowly drifted away with the current, while the tramps watched it and waved their tattered hats in farewell to the bravest twelve-year-old boy they had ever known.

CHAPTER XVII.

PLEASANT DRIFTINGS.

HOW really like a home their rude little old house-boat appeared to the boy, who had been lost in the woods and spent the night in a tramps' camp, and to the old man, who had passed the long hours in wandering up and down the lonely road, searching for his lost one. What comforts it contained, and with what a delightfully easy motion it glided down the sunlit river. Even Rusty seemed to feel that he was at home, and to recognize the place; for the moment he was taken into the cabin, he sprang up on Arthur's bunk, and nestled down at its foot, where the boy had prepared a bed for him two days before.

While Uncle Phin was getting ready the breakfast for which they were all so hungry, Arthur and Rusty, who had fully recovered his spirits, had a fine game of romp, during which the dog displayed so much intelligence, and performed so many funny tricks, as to completely win his young master's heart.

When breakfast was finished, Uncle Phin and Arthur sat on the cabin roof, under a bit of an awning that the former had contrived, and talked of their recent experience, while watching, with the delight of simple natures, the exquisitely beautiful scenery through which they were drifting. Between them, apparently appreciating it all as much as they, sat Rusty, contentedly wagging his tail, the little white tip of which seemed the emblem of perpetual motion. He had evidently transferred all his affection to Arthur, and the expression of his honest eyes, as he turned them upon his young master, was that of love and perfect confidence.

This day was but the first of many such, during which the Ark, with frequent stops, drifted down the quiet river, ever southward, and, as its occupants fondly hoped, ever getting nearer to the far-away home that they sought. They always tied up to the bank at night, and every now and then they spent several days in a place, while Uncle Phin sought odd jobs of work, by which he might earn a little money for the replenishing of their stock of provisions.

During one of these stops, at a place where there was a large hotel, in which a number of the summer guests lingered for the enjoyment of the autumn scenery, something very pleasant happened to them. A boy of just about Arthur's age and size, who was staying at the hotel, walked down to the river bank with his father. They were attracted by the quaint appearance of the Ark; and, on going close enough to look in at one of its open doors, were surprised to see that its occupants were an old negro and a barefooted boy, the first of whom was patching a small garment, while the other read aloud to him. The new-comers had little difficulty in forming the acquaintance of Arthur, Uncle Phin, and Rusty, or in learning their story.

In answer to Uncle Phin's anxious inquiry as to whether he knew of any work to be had in that neighborhood, the gentleman said he did not. Then, with a little hesitation, he added that if Arthur cared to come up to the hotel that evening, and read a story out of his book at a children's entertainment they were going to have, he would give him a dollar.

Glancing sadly down at his ragged clothes, the boy said he should like ever so much to do so, but did not see how he could.

Thereupon the gentleman, understanding the glance, said that his present costume was so picturesque that he wanted him to come just as he was, ragged, barefooted, and all. So Arthur went, being more proud of his ability to earn a whole dollar than he was ashamed of his appearance, and his reading was such a success that all the people were anxious to know who he was.

When it was over, the kind gentleman invited him to his room, where Arthur found a complete suit of the other boy's clothes, including shoes, stockings, and a round cap, which the gentleman said were for him, and insisted upon his putting on at once.

So the boy was again dressed, and made to feel like a young gentleman; and, when he reappeared down-stairs, nobody knew him, at first, for the one who had read to them.

The next day a gay party of these hotel guests chartered the Ark for an excursion, and drifted down the river on her, in company with Arthur and

Uncle Phin and Rusty, to a point about five miles below the village, where carriages were waiting to take them back. For this use of the boat they paid two dollars, besides leaving enough provisions behind them to last our friends for several days.

By the kind gentleman, who appeared greatly interested in their journey, Arthur and Uncle Phin were advised to sell their boat in Pittsburgh, as that would offer a better market than points farther on, and to take the cars from there.

So the whole month of October passed before the happy voyage was ended, and, late one afternoon in November, the Ark was moored at the mouth of a small creek on the outskirts of the city of Pittsburgh. It was a region of iron-works, of foundries, furnaces, and rolling mills, a place of noise and heat, and never-ending weariness. A dense cloud of black smoke hung low above it that still November evening, and, though the air was comparatively pure where the boat was moored, its pall-like presence seemed to cast a foreboding of evil days over the hearts of our travellers. As the darkness drew on, the smoke clouds were illumined by a strange, lurid, glare like that of a great volcano. It was a weirdly beautiful sight; but it filled them with uneasiness; and, after watching it for a while, they were glad to enter their cosey little cabin, and close it to all outside influences.

With heavy hearts they prepared and ate their evening meal; for there was only food enough left for a slender breakfast, and they had no money with which to purchase more. After supper they began seriously to consider their plans for the future, of which they had talked but vaguely thus far.

"Is n't it too bad that we can't go all the way in this boat?" said Arthur.

"It is so, Honey," replied Uncle Phin, "but dars no use er frettin. We'll go by de kyars and be dar in mos no time now."

"Do you think we'll get money enough to pay for riding on the cars, Uncle Phin?"

"Sho, Honey! You does n't know much about trabblin, dats a fac; why it don't take no money fer to ride on de kyars. De man wif de brass buttens, what owns 'em, jes gib you a lil ticket, and den you ride as long as you like."

Arthur was inclined to doubt this statement; but Uncle Phin was so positive, that he tried to believe it. The truth was that, on the only two railroad journeys he had ever taken in his life, Uncle Phin's tickets had been bought and paid for without his knowledge, and handed to the conductor by Mr. Dustin, together with the others for his little party. Then a conductor's check had been stuck in the old man's hat-band, and he had ridden unquestioned to his journey's end. Thus he was led to believe that railroads were built, and cars run upon them, for the free accommodation of all who were compelled by a hard fate to move restlessly from place to place, and he felt very grateful for the kindness thus extended.

"But Brace Barlow said we could sell the Ark for enough money to carry us the rest of the way when we got here, you told me so, yourself," said Arthur, "and what did he mean if it is n't going to cost anything?"

"Why, Honey, he mean to pay fer de grub we mus hab while we is a trabblin, an fer de candies and picshur books, what de boy in de kyars hans roun. You is jes nacherly 'bleeged to pay fer dem, ob cose. Yo fader allus done dat," answered the old man.

"Then we will have to sell the Ark to-morrow, I suppose," said Arthur, looking regretfully about the rude little cabin that had been so pleasant a home to him.

"To be shuah, Honey. We jes drap a bit furder down de ribber, inter de bizness place ob de city, fust ting in de mornin. Den we sell de boat, an take to de kyars what's boun fer ole Ferginny, an maybe by to-morrer night we is all safe an soun at Dalecourt."

"How much do you think we will get for the boat?"

"I don know per zackly, Honey. It'll be cordin ter de deman fer boats. Maybe five dollar, maybe ten. Depens on what dey is er fetchin," replied Uncle Phin, whose ideas as to the value of this sort of property were of the vaguest description.

As their backs were turned to the cabin window that was nearest the shore, neither Arthur nor Uncle Phin knew that, during this conversation, an evil-looking face was peering in at them, and that its owner was an attentive listener to all that they said.

Now, as they looked up, startled by an uneasy growl from Rusty, who had just detected the stranger's presence, and sprang barking toward the window, the face was hastily withdrawn, and appeared no more.

CHAPTER XVIII.

THE ARK IS STOLEN.

THE next morning, after eating the very last of their provisions, which they shared impartially with Rusty, they cast the Ark loose from its moorings, and allowed it to drift a mile or two down past the city water front. At length they reached a place of comparative quiet, amid the bewildering number of steamboats, tugs, and barges, by which they were now surrounded. It was just below a great bridge that spanned the river at this point, and here, after half an hour of anxiety and hard work, they finally succeeded in making their boat fast to the levee.

Then, not knowing what else to do, they waited patiently for some hours, in the hope that a customer would appear, and make them an offer for the Ark. But of all the hurrying throngs who passed the place, no one paid the slightest attention to them.

Uncle Phin had just decided that it would be necessary for him to go ashore, and in some way make it known that he had a boat for sale, when a stranger came walking briskly toward them, and sprang aboard.

Growling savagely, Rusty would have flown at the man, whom he recognized as the one who had looked into the cabin window the evening before, had not Arthur seized and held him.

"Good-morning," said the stranger, politely. "Fine watch dog you 've got there."

"Yes," replied Arthur, "he is; but I never knew him to want to bite anybody before."

"Oh, well," said the man, "he probably is n't used to city folks; but he will get over that. I came to ask if this boat is for sale."

"Of course it is," replied the boy, delightedly. "We have been hoping somebody would come along who wanted to buy it."

Then they showed the stranger all over the boat, explaining to him what an unusually fine craft it was, and, before long, had told him all he wanted to know of their history and plans.

He was a shabbily-dressed man; but they were

accustomed to seeing such people, and never for a moment mistrusted him when he said that he was looking for just that kind of a boat, in which to take his family to New Orleans for the winter. They only congratulated each other, on securing a customer so readily, by exchanging sundry significant looks and smiles behind his back.

At length he asked their price for the boat, and Uncle Phin, emboldened by his praise of the craft and evident desire to possess her, answered that, as boats seemed to be in pretty good demand, he thought this one ought to be worth twenty dollars.

"Nonsense!" exclaimed the stranger. "Twenty dollars! why, she is worth fifty, if she is worth a cent, and I could n't think of offering any less for her. Say fifty and we 'll call it a bargain."

Was there ever such a generous and honest man? Both Arthur and Uncle Phin thought there never was, as they gladly accepted this magnificent offer, and thanked him for it besides.

"Now," said the stranger, "business is business, and I should like to take possession of the boat at once; while I presume you are anxious to pursue your journey. If you will just step up-town with me to my bank, I will pay you the fifty dollars, and on the way I will show you the station of the railroad that goes to Virginia. Then we'll get a team to come down here for your baggage, and you'll be all right."

Neither Arthur nor the old negro could think of any particular baggage that they wished to carry with them, unless it was their bedding, and Uncle Phin's axe, and they told the stranger so. He said they might think of something else after they had got their money, and that at any rate they had better go up-town with him and secure it at once.

Arthur suggested that it might not be safe to leave the boat all alone, and proposed that Uncle Phin go for the money, while he and Rusty stayed behind to guard it.

"Oh, that's all right," said the stranger. "You never knew such honest folks as live round here. They would n't touch anything that did n't belong to them for the world. Besides I want you both to sign the bill of sale, and the receipt for the money."

So, after carefully closing the cabin doors and windows, the trusting old man, and the boy, ignorant as yet of the world's wickedness, accompanied the plausible stranger up-town. Arthur led Rusty by a bit of rope fastened to the leathern collar Uncle Phin had made for him, and had some difficulty in keeping him at a safe distance from the stranger, toward whom the dog seemed to have taken the greatest dislike. Moved by some impulse that he could not have explained, the boy had also taken his precious book from its shelf, at the last moment, and now carried it under his arm.

The stranger continued to be very polite and entertaining, as they walked through the crowded streets, and pointed out several places of interest, among others the railway station from which they were to take the train for Virginia.

They walked so far that Arthur began to grow tired, and was very glad when they at length entered a fine building, above the doorway of which he read the word "Bank" in large letters. Here both the old man and the boy were awed and bewildered by the imposing appearance of the interior into which they were ushered. They wondered at the number of desks, at which busy clerks sat writing behind a high and strong iron grating, and at the crowds of people who stood in long lines before the little windows in it, or passed hurriedly to and fro. Leading them to a retired corner, out of the throng, their guide bade them wait there for a few minutes, while he prepared the papers that it would be necessary for them to sign, and procured the fifty dollars. Then he mingled with the crowd of men about them, and disappeared.

For fifteen minutes or so, the attention of the old man and the boy was fully occupied by the novel scenes about them, and in keeping Rusty quiet. Then they began to watch anxiously for the stranger's return, and to grow somewhat uneasy over his non-appearance. When half an hour had passed, they were thoroughly alarmed, and began to walk up and down the crowded space, in front of the iron grating, peering wistfully into the faces of those who filled it, but without seeing him whom they sought.

At last a man, who had been closely watching their movements for some time, stepped briskly up to them, and laying a hand on Uncle Phin's shoulder said:

"Come, get out of here, old man. I've had my eye on you ever since you came in, and it's evident that you have no business here."

"But, boss, we 'se a lookin fer ——"

"Yes, I know you are looking for something you wont find here, so clear out, or else I'll have to put you out."

There was no use offering a further resistance to the detective, and so the next minute our two friends found themselves in the street, utterly bewildered, and not knowing which way to turn.

"What do you suppose it all means, Uncle Phin?" asked Arthur.

"Don know, Honey. Hit beat de ole man's 'sperience, and he don pear to know nuffin about hit."

"There is something wrong any way," said the boy, decidedly, "and I think the best thing we can do is to get back to the boat as quick as possible."

By inquiring they found out in which direction the river lay, and started to make their way to it as fast as they could. It was a long, weary walk, and when they finally reached the river, they spent nearly an hour searching and inquiring before they discovered the bridge near which the Ark had been left.

Now the boat was nowhere to be seen. In vain did they gaze up and down the river. They saw other house-boats, and many strange craft of all descriptions, but nothing that looked in the least like the one that had sheltered them for so long that it seemed like a very home. Then the truth began to dawn upon them. Their boat had been stolen, probably by the very man who had persuaded them to accompany him up-town, and then deserted them.

This belief was finally confirmed by a good-natured boatman of whom they made some inquiries, and who told them that the craft for which they were looking had been boarded and taken away by a couple of men more than two hours before. They had of course floated off down the river, and the boatman said the only thing for them to do was to hire a tug and go after her.

As this would have cost at least twenty dollars, and as they did not have a cent, it was of course out of the question. What were they to do? And what was to become of them?

It was now late in the afternoon, and in addition to being very tired they were very hungry. This latter unpleasant sensation was evidently shared by poor Rusty, who began to whine and look pleadingly up into his young master's face. To add to their misery, the dense smoke clouds that had been hanging lower and lower over the city now enveloped it entirely in damp, sooty folds, and a cold, drizzling rain began to fall.

Poor Arthur felt so utterly wretched that he would have cried, but for the remembrance that he was a Dale.

CHAPTER XIX.

PENNILESS WANDERERS IN A STRANGE CITY.

FRIENDLESS and penniless in a strange city; cold, wet, and hungry, with night near at hand. This was the present condition of little Prince Dusty and his Uncle Phin, as, realizing that they had been cruelly deceived and robbed by the stranger who had proposed to purchase their boat, they turned slowly away from the river. They knew not where to go; but, moved by the impulse that prompted them to seek shelter from the storm, they walked toward the buildings on a street that fronted the broad, sloping levee.

If they only had something to eat, their future might not seem so dark. Then they could talk over their situation and decide upon some plan. Now they could neither talk nor think of anything but the terrible hunger that turned their strength into weakness and drove every other thought from their minds.

It was now twenty-four hours since they had eaten a satisfactory meal; for their mouthful of breakfast had only whetted their appetite for more. Uncle Phin had known what hunger was before, and was thus somewhat prepared to bear its sufferings. Even Rusty's patient dog nature enabled him to suffer in silence, only revealing his misery by an occasional whine, and by appealing glances at his young master's face. To this same young master, however, the hunger wolf had never seemed so fierce, nor so terrible, as now. Many a night had the fatherless boy been sent to bed by his Aunt Nancy without any supper, and at such times he had been very hungry; but never had he imagined such a longing for food as he now experienced.

"Oh, Uncle Phin!" he moaned, "can't you think of any way to get something to eat? Just a loaf of bread or some crackers. It does n't seem as if I could stand it much longer."

"Well, Honey! my pore lil honey lamb! de ole man is a rackin his brain, an a projeckin, an a thinkin, and it 's mo'n likely he 'll strike up wif some plan dreckly. You see des yeah 'sperience hab kim up powerful sudden, an its umposserbilities hab tuk me by 'sprise. Now we might sell dat ar dorg Rusty fer ernough to buy a squar meal, ef we know'd whar to fin a pusson what wanted a dorg."

"Sell Rusty, Uncle Phin! Sell my dear little dog! Why, I'd starve first."

"Dats it! Dats jes de way I knowed 't would be," said the old man, shaking his head sadly. "Well, dars dat ar book ob yourn. We mighter——"

"My precious book, that the beautiful lady gave me!" cried the boy. "Why, Uncle Phin, that's worse than Rusty. I wouldn't give *it* up for anything in the world; not even for a great heaping plate of hot buckwheat cakes, with maple syrup on them."

"Or a fat possum roasted in a hole in de groun?" suggested the old man, his mouth watering at the thought.

"No, nor a beefsteak with baked sweet potatoes, and hot rolls," said the boy, who, under the circumstances, was certainly placing a high value on his book.

"Or a big dish er hominy smoking frum de kittle wif a plenty er pok gravy," added Uncle Phin eagerly, unable to conceive of anything more likely to tempt a hungry little boy than this.

"No, not for anything that was ever cooked, or ever will be, would I give up my own dear book," said Arthur stoutly.

They had found a temporary refuge from the rain in a doorway, and stood within its shelter during this exchange of the tantalizing thoughts uppermost in their minds. Nearly opposite to them was a street lamp that had just been lighted, and they watched the lamplighter enviously, as he shouldered his flaming torch and walked away, whistling merrily, doubtless to a home and supper.

Now, as in answer to Arthur's last remark, Uncle Phin was saying: "Well, den, Honey, I don see but what we 'se got er go hungry twel tomorrer, when maybe I kin git er job er wood sawin," there came a quick rush of feet on the wet flagging. Arthur turned to look at the flying figure, and gave a little cry of recognition, as the light from the street lamp fell on its face. At the same instant Rusty recognized in it his old persecutor, the boy with whom his young master had fought in the tramps' camp. With a growl he sprang forward. Arthur still held the end of his rope, and the dog's movement was so sudden that it nearly threw him down. As it was, he stumbled, and the precious book, so recently the subject of their conversation, fell to the sidewalk. The next moment another figure, and this time it was that of Sandy Grimes, the big tramp, rushed past, evidently in pursuit of his boy, and then all was again quiet.

Recovering himself, and taking a firmer hold on the rope that held the still excited Rusty, Arthur stepped forward and picked up his book of fairy tales. As he did so, a bit of dark paper, that seemed to fall from between its leaves, fluttered to the wet stones, and this the boy also picked up. Curious to see what it was, he held it to the light and uttered a cry of incredulous amazement.

It was a bank bill for five dollars; and, although Arthur did not know it at the time, it was the same one that his friend, Brace Barlow, had slipped between the leaves of the book on the night that he bade them farewell. Why Arthur had not discovered it long before, will always be a mystery that can only be accounted for by the fact that the book was a large one, and contained many stories, several of which he had not yet read. Between the leaves of one of these the bill had probably been all this time, and now, in the hour of the boy's sorest need, it came to him as though it were indeed a gift from the fairy god-mother who had written the inscription upon the fly-leaf of the volume.

Arthur's excitement was fully shared by Uncle Phin, though with the old man it assumed a quieter and more reverent form. He said: "De good Lawd seen de fix we was in, Honey, an He sen dis yeah in place ob er raben, fer our suppah. Dats what we 'se er wantin de mostes, an dats what we oughter to be gettin de fustes ting."

CHAPTER XX.

A RAILROAD EXPERIENCE.

TO Uncle Phin's proposition the boy fully agreed. Even Rusty seemed to comprehend that his young master's fortunes had taken a turn for the better; and, as they started up the street, in search of a place where they might obtain food, he danced about them barking joyously.

Before long they discovered a very small and humble bake shop, kept by a colored aunty, who looked almost as old as Uncle Phin; but who was as stout as he was thin, and whose head was covered by a Madras kerchief of vivid reds and yellows. She was not expecting any customers this stormy evening, and at first regarded the new-comers with suspicion, evidently fearing that they were about to appeal to her for charity. This, by the way, as they afterwards learned, was her name, "Aunt

Charity." She was, however, reassured by the sight of the five-dollar bill in Uncle Phin's hand, by the old man's extreme politeness, and by Arthur's honest blue eyes. In spite of his clothes being rain-soaked and mud-stained, he was so evidently a little gentleman, that she involuntarily dropped him a curtsey when, in winning tones, he said: "Please, ma'am, get us something to eat. We are nearly starved; but we have the money to pay for it, and I think we would like to have a good deal of most everything you have."

"To be suttinly, sah! To be suttinly, my pore lamb. You shall hab de bes Aunt Charity kin skeer up, dreckly," answered the old woman, dropping her curtsey, and gazing compassionately at the little fellow. "Ef you'd like to dry yo'sefs, while I 'se er gittin sumpin ready, yo'se welkum to step inter de kitchun, an set by de fire, Misto ―― " Here she paused and looked at Uncle Phin, as though waiting for him to complete her sentence by introducing himself.

"Phin Dale ob Dalecourt, Ferginny," said the old man, promptly, adding, "and dis my lil Marse Arthur Dale Dustin. We is a trabblin to his granpaw's, an is to take de kyars fo Dalecourt, soon as we is eatin our suppah."

As Aunt Charity had also spent the earlier days of her life in Virginia, a bond of sympathy was at once established between them, and she bustled about, with surprising agility for one of her size, to make the travellers comfortable. She had intended supplying their wants from the counter and well-filled shelves of her little shop; but, after they were comfortably seated in the friendly warmth of the kitchen stove, she decided to make a pot of tea, and then to fry a rasher of bacon with some eggs. Nor did she neglect their immediate wants, while preparing these things. Hunger was so plainly stamped on their faces, that it would have been cruel to keep them waiting a single minute before beginning to satisfy it. So she gave them each a big, shiny-topped bun, with currants in it, and when she saw Arthur breaking off a piece of his for Rusty, she immediately got another for the hungry dog.

What a pleasant contrast this cheerful, low-ceiled kitchen, with its glowing stove, presented to the cold, and wet, and darkness of the streets through which they were wandering so hopelessly but a few minutes before. How thoroughly Arthur and Uncle Phin appreciated its comforts, and what glances, expressive of gratitude and complete satisfaction, they exchanged as they sat on opposite sides of the stove, well back so as not to interfere with the ponderous but bustling movements of the mistress of the establishment.

In the darkest corner of the room was a high, calico-curtained bedstead, from beneath which projected one end of a low trundle-bed. In this could just be distinguished two little woolly heads, from which two pairs of wide-open black eyes gazed wonderingly at the strangers, and the busy scene about the stove.

When Uncle Phin inquired, with an air of well-feigned interest, if those were her children, Aunt Charity paused in her work for a moment, and, standing with arms akimbo, regarded them with great complacency, as she answered: "No, Misto Phin Dale, deys not my ownly chillun; but deys my gran'chillun, once remobed. You see deir maw, she my ole man's fustes wife's gal, by her fustes husban'. So when dey came to be twins an' orfuns at de same time, I wuz deir nex ob kin, an dey nacherly fell to my sheer ob de estate. Now, I 'se gwine gib 'em a eddicashun, and train 'em up fer de white-wash an kalsermine bizness."

Warm and dry, strengthened and refreshed by their supper, of which little Rusty had eaten his full share and would now have greatly preferred lying under the stove to going out into the stormy night, our travellers again set forth on their journey. Had Aunt Charity's mite of a house afforded a spare room she would have invited them to occupy it until morning; but it did not, and she had no place to offer them. Then, too, Uncle Phin was most anxious to start at once, now that they had money, in hopes that it would last until they reached their journey's end. So interested had Aunt Charity become in the young lad who was so bravely seeking a distant home in place of the one where he had been cruelly and unjustly treated—for Uncle Phin had told her the whole of Arthur's history,—that she at first refused to receive any pay for their supper. Both Arthur and Uncle Phin insisted so strongly that she should, that at length she consented to take twenty-five cents, but no more. She also forced into Uncle Phin's hands a paper bag full of rolls and cakes for Arthur just as they left, and stood in the doorway watching them until they were lost to sight in the shadows of the dimly lighted street.

Aunt Charity had given them directions for reaching the railway station, so that they had no trouble in finding it. Here they were quickly bewildered by the hurrying throngs of people and great trucks of baggage that were being trundled up and down the platform, the puffing and snorting of engines, and the dazzling white light of the electric lamps.

At last Uncle Phin ventured to address a man in a cap and blue coat, whom he took to be one of the railway officials.

"Please, sah," said the old man, bowing humbly and pulling at the brim of his tattered hat, "which ob de kyars is er gwine to Ferginny?"

"Which way are you bound?" asked the official, sharply. "East or west?"

Uncle Phin did not know.

"Let me see your tickets?"

Uncle Phin had none. "De man haint passen ob 'em roun yet," he said.

"Are you going to Richmond, Virginia?"

"Near by dar, sah! Clus on to it!" cried the old man, eagerly, delighted at hearing the familiar name.

"Well, then you want to take the first through train going east, and it won't be along till midnight."

With this the busy railroad man hurried on, leaving our friends gazing at each other in dismay. Midnight! and now it was only seven o'clock. What should they do and where should they go to pass those five hours? They did not dare go very far from the railway station, and so they wandered aimlessly about in the darkness near it, growing more weary, more wet, cold, and uncomfortable with each moment.

At length they paused before an empty freight car, one door of which was partly open. Why not seek shelter from the storm in it?

Nobody saw them as they climbed into the car, which they found to be half filled with sacks of cornmeal. On these they made themselves quite comfortable, and here they decided to wait patiently until the lighted clock on a tower above the station, which they could see from the car door, should tell them that it was nearly midnight. Of course they had no idea of going to sleep. That would never do; for they must watch the clock. How slowly its hands crept round. Arthur resolutely turned his eyes away from it, determined not to look again for at least half an hour. When satisfied that that length of time had elapsed, he glanced at its round yellow face, only to find that barely five minutes had passed. He spoke of this to Uncle Phin, but received no answer. The old man was fast asleep.

"Poor Uncle Phin!" said the boy to himself. "He must be very tired, and I won't wake him till it's time to go."

So Arthur watched the lighted clock until it looked like a moon, and then he rubbed his eyes to make sure that it was not winking and laughing at him. And then—and then he too was fast asleep, with one arm thrown about Rusty's neck, and the only sounds to be heard were the patter of rain on the roof of the motionless freight car, and the regular breathing of its three tired occupants.

An hour later two men, carrying lanterns and wearing rubber coats that glistened with the wet, came along and paused before the freight car. One of them consulted a way bill. "Yes, this is it," he said. "No. 201, corn-meal for Harrisburg. Six sacks to be left at Arden. That's all right. Shut her up, Joe. It was mighty careless of those fellows to leave the door open."

Then Joe pushed the heavy door to, with a slam. It fastened with a spring lock, and the men with the lanterns walked away to look up the rest of their train. A little later an engine came rolling softly along the wet track to where the car stood. There was a bump, a rattle of coupling pins and links, a swinging of lanterns, and the car was drawn away, past the multitude of little red, and green, and yellow lights twinkling through the rain and darkness like big fire-flies, and marking the switches.

The car was hauled and pushed hither and thither, and others were attached to it, until at length a long train was made up. The great locomotive panted, eager to be off, and its hot breath made little clouds of fleecy steam, that were edged with flame by the glow from its open-mouthed furnace. The brakemen were at their posts on the slippery tops of the cars; the caboose at the rear end of the train looked warm and comfortable. The red lights, shining like angry eyes, were hung in position on its sides near the rear end, and freight train No. 15 was in readiness for a start.

The conductor came from the Train Despatcher's office with a thin sheet of yellow paper, on which were written his orders, in his hand.

"No tramps on board to-night, are there, Joe?" he said to his head brakeman.

"No, sir, not a sign of one. I've looked carefully everywhere. It's too wet for 'em to travel, I reckon."

"All right. Let her go."

Then the conductor swung his glistening lantern, the engineer pulled the throttle, and Freight No. 15 moved slowly out into the darkness. Its first stop was at Arden, where it was to side-track and await the passing of the New York Limited. Here too were to be left six sacks of meal.

As Brakeman Joe unlocked and pushed open the door of car No. 201, and the light of his lantern flashed into its dark interior, it fell upon something that caused him to start and exclaim:

"Great Scott! the tramps are travelling after all, and here they are. A dog too! Well, if that is n't cold cheek!"

CHAPTER XXI.

CARRIED OFF IN A FREIGHT CAR.

BRAKEMAN JOE did not love tramps. His regular work was hard enough, goodness knows; and when, in addition to it, he had to make a thorough examination of the whole train at every stopping-place, peering, by the light of his lantern, between and underneath the cars for tramps, who might be stealing a ride, he felt that he had good cause to dislike them. Sometimes he had hard tussles before dislodging them from their perches and roosts, and many an ugly blow had he received while performing this duty. Joe had, therefore, learned to deal very promptly, not to say roughly, with this portion of the travelling public whenever he found them on or in the cars under his charge.

On this particular night he had made sure, before starting, that there was not a single tramp on the train, and had in consequence been anticipating a comparatively easy trip. And now he had, as he supposed, discovered a whole nest of them snugly stowed away in car No. 201. A dog too! It was aggravating, and, under the circumstances, it is not to be wondered at that he hustled them out of there without much regard to their feelings.

Both Arthur and Uncle Phin had been suddenly awakened, and greatly alarmed, when Brakeman Joe first slammed and locked the door of the car in which they had taken refuge from the storm. They had a confused idea that they had been asleep, though for how long they could not tell, and now they could no longer see the lighted clock above the railway station. It might even be midnight, and time for their train to come along for all they knew. They shouted, and kicked against the locked door, and Rusty barked; but all in vain. The conductor and Brakeman Joe had walked away before these noises began, and there was no one else to hear them.

Then the engine came and pushed and pulled the car about until they had not the slightest idea of the direction in which they were moving. It might be forward or backward, east or west, for all they could tell. Nor was their situation improved when the train, of which car No. 201 finally formed a part, pulled out of the railway yard, and started on its long journey. They had no idea which way it was going, and Arthur could have cried as he reflected that they might be travelling in exactly the opposite direction from that they wished to take, and might be carried hundreds of miles before their car door was again unlocked. As he could not do this, because he was a Dale, he only hugged little Rusty, and tried to be comforted by Uncle Phin's assurances "Dat de good Lawd was er gwine ter keer for dem, jes like He did fer de sparrers, whose hairs was all counted so as dey shouldn' fall to de groun."

Arthur's unhappiness was increased by the fact that he could nowhere feel his precious book. It had slipped from his grasp as he slept, and now was nowhere to be found. Thus the first stage of their journey by rail was a most unhappy one, and they were glad to forget their sorrows in the sleep that again overcame them a few minutes before the train made its first stop.

The Arden station was a very small one, in a lonely place, with no houses near it. It was only a platform with a freight shed at one end, and a more forlorn place for a stranger to be left on a dark, stormy night, could hardly be imagined. Arthur and Uncle Phin were not conscious of the train stopping here, and were only awakened from their troubled sleep by the light from Brakeman Joe's lantern flashing in their faces. They were just sitting up and gazing at him, in a bewildered way, when this energetic young man hustled them out of the car in his roughest manner. It was so rough, in fact, that poor Uncle Phin, impelled by a violent push, slipped on the wet platform, and fell heavily. He struck one of his knees such a painful blow that, for a few moments, he was unable to rise, and lay there groaning.

"Are n't you ashamed of yourself to treat an old man so!" cried Arthur to Brakeman Joe, as with flashing eyes and quivering lips he sprang to his companion's side, and endeavored to assist him to his feet.

"Well, what business has the old tramp got to be stealing a ride on my train?" replied the brakeman, sulkily, though at the same time bending over Uncle Phin and helping him up.

He was not a bad-hearted young man, this Brakeman Joe; but he was overworked, and much bothered by tramps. Generally he was good-natured, and was especially kind and gentle with old people, for he had an old father at home of whom he was the sole support, and to whom he was devoted. He had not noticed, in the dim light, that Uncle Phin was old and white-headed. He had only regarded him as a tramp, who, as everybody knows, is apt to be young and strong, and well able to perform the labor that he refuses to undertake out of sheer laziness. So now he helped the prostrate figure to its feet, said he hoped the old fellow was not much hurt, and then returned to his task of dragging the six sacks of meal, that were to be left at Arden, from the car.

"What's the matter here, Joe?" asked the conductor of the train, stepping up at this moment.

"Only a couple of stowaways that I found stealing a ride in this car," was the answer.

"Tramps, eh?" said the conductor, sharply, flashing the light from his lantern upon the two trembling figures who stood behind him. "A dog, too," he continued, "and I'll warrant they stole it. I've a mind to take it in payment for their ride. If this was a town I'd have you fellows arrested and locked up in less than no time. You, and all your kind, ought to be killed off for the good of the country. As it is I'll leave you here to soak in the rain for the rest of the night, and perhaps some of the worthlessness will be washed out of you by morning. Hello! what's this?"

Here the conductor stooped and picked up a small object over which Brakeman Joe had stumbled, and which he had sent flying out on to the platform.

It was a book, and the conductor picked it up, wondering where it could have come from. "'Andersen's Fairy Tales,'" he read aloud, holding it up to his lantern. "The very book my little Kitty was asking me to get for her only the other day! Well, if this is n't a find!" Then, turning to the fly-leaf, he read aloud: "To Prince Dusty, from——"

Here he was interrupted by Arthur, who sprang forward, and, stretching out his hand for the book, cried: "Please, sir, it's mine; and I should feel dreadfully to lose it, and we are n't tramps, and did n't mean to steal a ride. We got locked in by accident, and we have money enough to pay for everything, and oh! please don't leave us here in this lonely place."

The conductor stared at the boy in amazement. "Well, you do look like a 'little Dusty' sure enough, though I can't say that you are exactly what I should have fancied a Prince was. Who are you, anyway? And where do you want to go to?"

Then Arthur, who was completely covered with white dust from the meal sacks on which he had been sleeping, told the conductor, in as few words as possible, of the object of their journey, and how they happened to be locked into car No. 201. He finished by repeating that they had money, and would willingly pay for the privilege of riding further on the train, provided it was bound east. This last question was asked most anxiously, for as yet the boy had not the slightest idea of where they were.

"Bound east!" exclaimed the conductor. "Of course we are, and there goes the 'New York Limited' now." As he spoke, an express train, of heavy vestibuled cars, thundered past them, with a roar and a crash, at such tremendous speed that in a second it was gone, and its two red eyes, looking backward, seemed to wink mockingly at the snail-like freight train, as they were whisked out of sight.

"Now," said the conductor as the roar of the express dying away permitted his voice to be again heard, "I'll tell you what I will do. You say you are not tramps, and did n't mean to stow away in that car, and that you have money enough to pay for your trip. That all may be so, and it may not. At any rate I have n't time to investigate your story now, for we must pull out of here at once. So you and the old man and the dog just tumble into that caboose, and I'll carry you along a bit further. We'll see about paying for the trip when you decide how far you want to go, and you shall read a story out of your book to Brakeman Joe and me, to pay for the ride you have already had. But mind," he added threateningly as Arthur began to thank him, "if I find that you have been telling me any lies, I'll have you arrested and locked up in the very first town we come to."

CHAPTER XXII.

SAVING THE KEYSTONE EXPRESS.

CONDUCTOR TOBIN, of freight No. 15, was one of the biggest-hearted and most generous men on the road. In fact it was largely owing to this that he had not long ago been promoted from a freight to a passenger train. He could not bear the thought of taking a place from any of his friends, whom he thought needed it more than he did. So he always held back, and let them step up over his head, and rejoiced with them in their good fortune, and said he would take his turn next time. He had a wife and one little girl about Arthur's age, whose name was Katherine, but who was called "Kitty" for short; and, though the conductor's pay was small, they managed to make both ends meet, and lived very happily in Harrisburg, in a little cottage that they only rented, but which it was their great desire to own, some day. It was so conveniently situated, not far from the railroad, and yet in such a nice part of the town that Mrs. Tobin often said to Conductor Tobin that they could not find one more to their liking, if they should look for a hundred years, and Conductor Tobin agreed with her.

Like Brakeman Joe, the only persons with whom Conductor Tobin had no patience, and upon whom he was very severe whenever they came in his way, were tramps. In the present case he was pleased with the sweet, honest face of little "Prince Dusty," a name that struck his fancy most happily. It seemed a proof of the truthfulness of Arthur's claims, that he possessed, and evidently valued, the very book for which his little girl had expressed a desire. Thus he became favorably inclined toward our travellers, and offered to help them on with their journey.

So it happened that, when freight No. 15 pulled slowly and heavily out from the Arden siding, Arthur and Uncle Phin and Rusty, instead of being left behind on the storm-beaten platform, were comfortably seated about the little round stove in the caboose, enjoying its grateful warmth and very happy over their good fortune.

Soon after starting, Conductor Tobin and Brakeman Joe entered the caboose, and sat down for a chat with their guests. Uncle Phin was too fully occupied in nursing his bruised knee to enter very heartily into the conversation; but Arthur so easily sustained his share of it, that the trainmen were delighted with his intelligence and ready wit. After he had told them all that he could about himself, he began to ask them questions, whereby he gained much information concerning railroad business in general, and the running of trains in particular. They allowed him to climb up into the cupola of the caboose, through the four windows of which he could look out into the night, ahead, behind, and on both sides. Then they showed him their red and white lanterns, and set of flags, and explained their uses. He thus learned that, if any accident happened to their train, it would be the conductor's first duty to send a brakeman back on the track to wave a red lantern, and warn approaching trains of the danger ahead.

"Would a train always stop if a red lantern was waved across the track ahead of it?" asked Arthur.

"Of course it would," was the answer, "for if it did n't it would get into trouble."

Brakeman Joe even went so far as to initiate the boy into the mysteries of his own peculiar department. Of course he did not invite him to walk over the wet roofs of the moving train, in order to show him how the brakes of the freight cars were set up; but he gave him a lesson on the platform of the caboose that answered every purpose.

Then the trainmen brought out their tin lunch pails, and from their contents, together with those of the paper bag so thoughtfully provided by Aunt Charity, the merry party of five, for of course the always-hungry Rusty was included in it, made a hearty midnight supper.

Freight No. 15 had stopped several time to drop or pick up loaded cars; but, as yet, nothing had been said about leaving the guests behind, or about Arthur reading a story in payment for the earlier portion of their ride. At length, when they were toiling slowly up a long, heavy grade, for they were now climbing the western slope of the Alleghany Mountains, Conductor Tobin claimed the fulfilment of this promise, and Arthur willingly undertook to read the story of "The Wild Swans." Brakeman Joe was at his post in the cupola on look-out, so of course he could not be expected to listen to the reading. Nor could the conductor hear very well, above the roar of the train, though the boy strove to read loudly and clearly. At length, as it was evident that he was straining his voice, and also that he was growing very sleepy, kind-hearted Conductor Tobin gently took the book from his hands, and bade him lie down on a sort of long bench, covered with a cushion and a blanket, that ran along one side of the caboose, while he finished the story for himself.

Here, with Rusty nestled close beside him, the tired boy quickly fell asleep, while Uncle Phin nodded and dozed in a big arm-chair beside the stove, and the only sounds heard were the panting of the locomotive, and the rattle of the heavy train as it toiled slowly up the steep grades.

Somewhere near the summit a stop was made for water. During it both Conductor Tobin and Brakeman Joe went to the forward end of the long train for a chat with the engineer. They were still talking when it was time to start ahead, and both men jumped into the cab for a moment that they might finish what they were saying. Then they began to make their way back toward the caboose, walking as quickly and surely over the swaying roofs of the cars as though they had been on solid ground.

It had ceased to rain; but thick, damp mist clouds, were driving over the mountains, and they at first thought this was the reason why they did not see the green lights, that should show in the back of the red caboose lanterns. Then they became anxious, and quickened their steps. When they reached the end of the train their worst fears were realized. The caboose was no longer there.

The engineer, happening to look back, saw their swinging lanterns. A sharp, imperative whistle blast called for brakes. For a few moments there was a harsh grinding of the iron brake shoes against iron wheels, and then the train came to a standstill. As it did so Conductor Tobin ran breathlessly up to the locomotive, shouting: "Back down to the tank! Side-track the train, and run your engine back after the caboose. It's broke loose and gone down the grade! Number 17 is coming up behind us! There is n't one chance in ten thousand but what there'll be a collision! We've got to take that one though, and do what we can."

Long before he finished speaking Conductor Tobin was in the cab, and the train was backing rapidly toward the siding. Brakeman Joe had run back to the little green light at its end, unlocked and thrown over the lever, so that now a "flying switch" was made, and, while the train ran in on the siding, the locomotive, previously cut loose from it, still stood on the main track. Again the lever was thrown over, the green light, denoting that the main track was open, swung into place, and the engine seemed to give a great bound as it plunged swiftly down the grade in pursuit of the runaway caboose.

In the meantime Arthur had been suddenly awakened from his nap by a peculiar jarring jerk that accompanied the starting of the train, and by a loud barking from Rusty. For an instant the caboose stood still, though he could hear the other cars in motion, then it began to move backwards; at first very slowly, but increasing its speed with each moment. Although he did not yet realize in the least what had happened, the boy felt uneasy, and stepping to the door he looked out. Even to his inexperienced eye the situation was clear at a glance.

A coupling-pin had broken, and the caboose was running away down the steep grade the train had just climbed.

"Quick, Uncle Phin!" he shouted, "come here quick!" and the old man, hobbling to the door, found the boy exerting all of his strength upon the iron brake wheel.

Together they tugged and strained at it until at length they got the brake set, after a fashion. Of course not as Brakeman Joe's powerful arms could have done it, but so that its iron shoes ground with considerable force against the wheels.

At first it did not seem to have the slightest effect, and the car still rushed at a fearful speed down the mountain side, whirling around the sharp curves with sickening lurches that nearly threw its passengers off their feet.

Suddenly a new terror was added to the situation. From down in the valley came the shrill whistle of an approaching train, and they knew it was climbing the grade toward them on the same track. Now their runaway car struck a short place of comparative level, and its speed seemed to slacken.

If they could only set that brake up one more notch! It seemed impossible; but they did it, and the red sparks began to fly from the grinding wheels.

They were certainly going slower, and, at last, on the beginning of an abrupt curve, they stopped. Another hundred feet would have sent them flying down the steepest grade of the mountain.

Arthur bade Uncle Phin take one of the two red lanterns left in the car and swing it from the front platform. Then, with the other in his hand, he jumped to the track, and ran at the top of his speed around the curve ahead of them. He was not a second too soon, for within a hundred yards of the caboose he was nearly blinded by the sudden glare of an approaching headlight. Standing steadily in the middle of the track he swung his danger signal to and fro, until he could feel the hot breath of the approaching monster, and then he sprang aside.

Its powerful air brakes were already at work, and the "Keystone Express," filled with sleeping passengers, came to a standstill within a few feet of the runaway caboose, just as the engine from the freight train bumped softly against it from the other direction.

As Conductor Tobin picked Arthur up in his

STANDING STEADILY IN THE MIDDLE OF THE TRACK HE SWUNG HIS
DANGER SIGNAL TO AND FRO. (*Page* 180.)

arms and carried him back to the caboose the tears were streaming down his face, and he said: "God bless you, lad! You've done a thing this night the oldest trainman on the road might be proud of doing."

CHAPTER XXIII.

CROSSING THE ALLEGHANIES.

So little "Prince Dusty," by remembering what he had been taught, and having the common-sense to put it into practice, was able to prevent a terrible disaster. Some boys of his age would have been so frightened at finding themselves in a runaway car, plunging madly down a mountain-side, that they would have become panic-stricken and utterly powerless to help themselves or others. They would have, as people say, lost their heads; but Arthur was not one of the kind who lose their heads. He had been sensibly brought up by his practical father, and taught to face emergencies coolly and calmly. Young as he was, he had learned to stop and think "What is the best thing to be done?" and then to do it promptly to the very best of his ability. It does not take long to think.

If the brain is clear and steady, a great many thoughts can flash through it in a second; and one moment thus spent is worth a lifetime of thoughtless action.

It would be absurd to claim that Arthur had not been frightened on this occasion. He had never been so frightened in his life, and it is to be hoped that he never will be again; but he was too brave a boy to allow his fright to obtain control of him. Now that the time for being cool and calm, and for prompt action, had passed, he felt weak and faint, and was very glad to be picked up and borne tenderly back to the caboose, in Conductor Tobin's strong arms. There Uncle Phin was waiting to throw his arms about his "lil Marse," and to "tank de good Lawd" for letting him be the brave, splendid boy that he was.

The runaway caboose was hauled up to where the rest of its train was waiting on the siding for it, and the "Keystone Express" followed slowly. Here it stopped for a few minutes, while its engineer and conductor, and the conductors of the sleeping-cars, all crowded into the caboose to see and shake hands with the boy who had saved their lives, and to thank him with trembling voices. They wanted Arthur and Uncle Phin and Rusty to go with them, and travel, surrounded by every comfort and luxury that their train could afford; but Arthur said he would rather stay where he was. This decision made Conductor Tobin and Brakeman Joe very happy, for they were so proud of their young "railroad man," as they called him, that they could not bear the thought of parting with him.

So, with many a full-hearted "God bless you!" and "We'll not forget you in a hurry," the trainmen of the "Keystone Express" went back to their places, and it rolled away over the mountains, without its sleeping passengers being any the wiser for what had happened. Nor did they ever know of the danger they had escaped; for passengers on railway trains are never told, if it can be helped, of their narrow escapes from accidents. It might make them timid about riding in the cars.

Only one passenger knew. He was an elderly gentleman, who, unable to sleep, had been lying in a lower berth, gazing out into the darkness through his uncurtained window. He knew of the sudden and unusual stopping of the train, had seen the swinging lanterns, and had noticed the engineer and conductors of his own train crowding into the caboose of Freight No. 15. When the express was once more in motion, he called the porter of the sleeping-car, and made him tell all he knew of what had taken place.

When the story was finished, the elderly gentleman sighed regretfully, and said he wished he had known of it in time to go and see that boy for himself. He had no boys of his own, and had never cared much for them; but recent circumstances had caused him to change his mind, and long for one. He had even come to regard all boys with interest, and now wished he might have known the brave little fellow whose courage and promptness of action had, in all probability, saved his life.

After the express had passed on, and Freight No. 15 was again pounding heavily along over the steel rails, Conductor Tobin and Brakeman Joe sat by the little caboose stove and talked over the events of the past half hour. Arthur lay quietly on the blanket-covered bench, with Rusty curled up at his feet, and Uncle Phin, sitting close beside him, held one of his hands, as though fearful of losing him.

The two men told each other what a wonderful thing it was that these stowaways had chosen their particular train, and how thankful they were that they had not left them at Arden, as they at first intended. They could not tire of praising the boy for remembering what they had just taught him, and for being so ready to act upon it. They praised Uncle Phin, too, for his share of the night's work, and even little Rusty was petted and praised for barking to wake Arthur when the caboose broke loose.

Brakeman Joe said that the boy was so evidently cut out for a railroad man that it would be a pity if he should ever try to become anything else. He even went so far as to offer Arthur and Uncle Phin a home with his old father, promising to teach the former all he knew of railroading, and to get him a place as water-boy on a passenger train.

Arthur gratefully declined this offer, and said he thought they had better keep on with their journey to the home in which he belonged. At the same time a genuine love for railroads and everything connected with them, even including their dangers, had entered his heart that night, and he determined that some day he would not only be a railroad man, but a famous one.

They had now passed the summit of the Alleghanies, and day was dawning. As the night mists rolled away, and the magnificent panorama of mountain, hill, and valley began to unfold beneath them, Arthur climbed up into the cupola to watch it. He had never witnessed so glorious a sunrise as that now flashed back by the clear waters of the Juniata, which laughed and rippled beside the track. As he drew in long breaths of the fresh mountain air and gazed on the marvellous beauty of the ever-widening landscape, the mere fact of being alive and able to enjoy it all filled him with happiness.

During the morning Freight No. 15 rumbled heavily across the Susquehanna River and into the beautiful old city of Harrisburg, the proud capital of one of the greatest and wealthiest States of the Union. Here it was turned over to a new crew of trainmen, while Conductor Tobin, Brakeman Joe, and the others who had brought it thus far were at liberty to seek their homes and a well-earned rest.

Conductor Tobin insisted upon taking our travellers home with him, and, though Brakeman Joe would gladly have had them as his guests, he was obliged to yield to the claims of his superior officer.

So they all went to the neat little cottage, not far from the railroad, where, when warm-hearted Mrs. Tobin learned from her husband what Arthur and Uncle Phin and Rusty had done, she took the boy at once into her arms and heart, and shook hands with the old negro, and petted the dog, and said that her house was honored by having such distinguished guests under its roof. Then she prepared an extra fine dinner for the occasion, and even little Rusty was allowed to sit at the table and have his share of it, "just like folks," as Mrs. Tobin said.

After dinner Arthur won Kitty's heart by reading stories to her out of his precious book, and Uncle Phin won it by carving toys out of bits of soft pine with his jack-knife, and Rusty won it by performing all his tricks and playing with her.

That evening Conductor Tobin produced a railroad folder that contained a map. On this they traced out the course of the journey yet to be undertaken to the point on the James River not far from Richmond, Virginia, where Uncle Phin said Dalecourt was located. When their route had been carefully marked in red ink the map was entrusted to Arthur for their future guidance.

CHAPTER XXIV.

A BRAVE STRUGGLE WITH POVERTY.

THE following day Conductor Tobin introduced his guests to a freight conductor on the Northern Central road, who, when he had heard their story, willingly consented to carry them on his train, which was to go out that night, as far as Baltimore.

This he did; and when they got there, they had not spent one cent of the money with which they had left Pittsburgh, and yet they had accomplished two thirds of their journey.

As the weather was pleasant, they decided to walk from Baltimore, at least as far as Washington. So the Northern Central conductor set them down at a small station just outside the city limits of Baltimore. Then, after pointing out the direction they were to take, he bade them good-by, and left them to pursue their journey on foot, with light hearts and a firm faith that they would speedily accomplish it.

From the very outset of this walk Arthur began to realize the value of the information given him long before, in the tramps' camp on the Alleghany, regarding their peculiar signs, as inscribed on fences and gate-posts. While he and Uncle Phin had some money, it was so very little for the long journey still ahead of them, that they must use every means possible to save it. They did not expect to live at first-class hotels during their travels, or even in cheap lodging-houses. They only hoped to obtain permission to sleep in barns, or under haystacks if nothing better offered, and to buy their food of such farmers' wives as would let them have what was left over from their own tables.

Therefore it became very important for them to know who were the liberal, good-natured people along their route, and which were the ones from whose doors they would be chased away by dogs, or threatened with shot-guns. To discover this Arthur kept a sharp look-out for signs by the roadside.

It was surprising, now that he began to look for them, and to discover for himself where to look, how many he found. There was hardly a dwelling along the way but what had the character of its inmates denoted by rude chalk marks on some conspicuous object in its immediate vicinity. So by applying only at the houses whose signs were favorable, they got along very nicely for three days. They were allowed to sleep in comfortable barns each night, and had several meals given to them without charge, though they always offered to pay for what they received. Thus, on the fourth day, when they expected to reach Washington, they had spent but one dollar of their little store.

As neither of them was used to walking, and as to Uncle Phin's rheumatic stiffness of limb was now added a severe pain in the knee that had been injured by falling on the platform at Arden, their progress was very slow. It was so slow, in fact, that Arthur began to despair of ever completing their long journey on foot, and to wonder if no other means of travel could be found.

He was so busily thinking over the several plans that proposed themselves, on the evening of that fourth day, that he hardly paid any attention to the great white dome of the Capitol at Washington that, looming high above the city, marked the end of this stage of their journey. Nor did he pay much attention to the black clouds gathering overhead, until Uncle Phin, who was hobbling painfully along beside him, said: "We 'se er gwine hab a storm, Honey, an I spec hits comin down rambumptious." As he spoke there came a wild gust of wind accompanied by a flurry of rain.

They were on such a lonely stretch of road that there was no house in sight, and only a haystack in a neighboring field offered the slightest shelter. So they hurried to it, and burrowing under its leeward side, found there comparative protection from the storm, which they hoped would be of short duration.

But it lasted all night, with the wind shifting and blowing from every quarter; so that, after long hours of sleepless misery, the gray dawn found them soaked to the skin by the pitiless rain, faint with hunger, and shivering with cold.

With the first daylight they tried to move on in search of a house; but when poor Uncle Phin attempted to rise from his cramped position, he sank back with a groan. His injured knee had swollen and stiffened during the night, so that every effort to move it now gave him excruciating pain. He was entirely helpless; and the twelve-year-old boy, upon whom this new responsibility had so suddenly fallen, was, for a few moments, overwhelmed by it. Then he rallied bravely, and, saying, "I am going for help, Uncle Phin, but I'll be back just as quick as I can," he started on a run across the sodden field, toward the road.

In less than half an hour he returned with a team that he had discovered on its way to the city. Its driver agreed to take them as far as he went for two dollars, which sum Arthur gladly promised him. He would have given everything he possessed, and even willingly have resigned his prospects of finding a home, for the sake of getting his dear old friend to some shelter in which he could have warmth and food.

With great difficulty they got Uncle Phin into the wagon, where he lay with his head in Arthur's lap. Two hours later they were established in an humble negro boarding-house, to which the driver of the wagon had taken them. Here they could have a small but neat and well-warmed room for a dollar a week, payable in advance.

Procuring a cup of hot tea and some broth for Uncle Phin, besides food for himself and Rusty, completely exhausted Arthur's slender stock of money. So, when he had got Uncle Phin to bed, and seen that he was as comfortable as possible, the brave, tired little fellow started out into the strange city to try and earn some more.

That day he made twenty-five cents, by holding a horse for several hours, while its rider was attending to some business in one of the public buildings. Then, for several days, his fortunes fluctuated; on one of them he made a whole dollar by running errands, holding horses, carrying parcels for ladies who were shopping, and by doing, cheerfully and faithfully, from morning to night, everything that offered, no matter how hard or disagreeable it was. On other days he made nothing.

At length a piece of good fortune befell him. The holiday season was drawing near, and the business of the retail stores was greatly increased. The proprietor of one of them, who had noticed this cheerful little errand-boy waiting for odd jobs in front of his store, finally offered him regular work, for a few weeks, at fifty cents a day. For this he was always to be on hand to open the doors of carriages, carry parcels for shoppers to the horse-cars, and make himself generally useful outside the store.

In the meantime, poor Uncle Phin, stricken with rheumatic fever, lay suffering and groaning in his bed through the long, lonely days of several weeks, before he was again able to hobble about.

During these weeks of toil, suffering, and anxiety, little Rusty was Arthur's constant companion and sole comforter, and the boy grew to love him better than anything on earth, except Uncle Phin. In going to and fro from his work each day, he passed a certain house, in which lived a gentleman who was very fond of dogs. This gentleman noticed Rusty, and took such a fancy to him that he several times offered to buy him. Arthur steadily refused these offers, until at length, when Christmas was past, and there was no more work for him at the store. Then he went to the gentleman's house, and trying to speak bravely, but with quivering lips and tear-filled eyes, told him he might have the dear little dog for two tickets to Richmond.

Uncle Phin was again able to travel, and intensely anxious to continue their journey, so as to reach his old home "befo de dawn ob de New Yeah." Arthur's travels had taught him that railroad tickets cost money; but with all his efforts and self-denials, he had been unable to save anything from his scanty earnings. So, for Uncle Phin's sake, he finally decided to sacrifice his dear Rusty, if by so doing he could obtain the means of getting to Richmond.

The gentleman gladly, and without asking any questions, accepted this strange offer, and sent a servant to procure the required tickets. Then the poor little fellow, after giving Rusty a long parting hug, ran home, with a heavy heart, and a suspicious moisture glistening in his eyes.

The next day they travelled in the cars to Richmond, and the mere knowledge that he was once more in old Virginia, seemed to infuse new life into Uncle Phin. Without a moment's delay, they started to walk the ten miles of rough, frozen road that lay between the city and Dalecourt.

The old man's strength lasted wonderfully, but it gave out when they were still two miles from their destination; and, tottering to the doorway of a dilapidated and deserted cabin, that stood on the roadside, he declared that he could go no farther, and begged his boy companion to go on without him.

To this Arthur would not listen for a moment; but, helping the old man into the cabin, he declared they could rest there very comfortably until morning. Then he gathered a quantity of sticks, broken branches, and small logs, which he piled in the big fireplace that filled one end of the cabin's single room. He had just one match, but it did its duty, and soon a cheerful blaze was roaring up the old earthen chimney.

Grateful for its warmth, and for even this poor shelter, they prepared to pass, as best they might in this lonely place, the last night of the old year. There were no doors or windows to the cabin, so that everything they did might be plainly seen by any chance passers along that wintry road.

Arthur still had his book of fairy tales; and, as darkness set in, the old man begged him to read " jes one lilly story " from it, to help them forget their wretchedness. So, sitting in the brightest glow of the firelight, the boy bent his brave, careworn young face over the pages, and read the touching story of " The Little Match-Girl."

Her situation and theirs were so much alike, that the story seemed very real to him; and as he started at the sound of a rustle behind him just as he closed the book, he looked up, almost expecting to see some beautiful vision. Nor was he disappointed. A dainty, richly-clad figure stood in the doorway. As the boy lifted his eyes he uttered a cry of mingled fear, amazement, and joy. The face into which he was looking was that of the beautiful lady who had given him this precious book, and who had written in it "To Prince Dusty, from his Fairy Godmother."

THE FAIRY GODMOTHER FINDS PRINCE DUSTY. (*Page* 198.)

CHAPTER XXV.

FINDING A HOME.

BEFORE Arthur could recover in the slightest from his bewilderment at this wonderful and undreamed-of appearance of his beautiful lady in such a place, she stepped forward and caught him in her arms. "Oh, my little Prince Dusty! My dear little Prince Dusty!" she cried. " Where have you been? How did you get here? Do you know that I am your cousin? Your own cousin, Harriet Dale, and that I live at Dalecourt? I never was so utterly amazed in my life as I am to find you here! We knew that you had left the Dustins; but nobody could tell where, or how, you had gone. And to think that you should have come to Dalecourt! I don't see how you ever found the way! It is the very most wonderful thing I ever heard of! How did you get here? But, no matter now. How thoughtless I am to stand here asking all these questions. You look frozen and starved, poor child, and the first thing is to get you home as quickly as possible. Who is this with you? Not Uncle Phin! Surely not the Uncle Phin who used to be so good to me when I was a little girl?"

"Yes, Miss Hatty," answered the old man, who had scrambled stiffly to his feet upon her entrance, and now stood with his white head uncovered, laughing and crying at the same time. "Hit am de same ole Unc Phin, an he tank de good Lawd he is lib to see a shuah nough Dale once mo. He done bring lil Marse home, Miss Hatty. Hits been powerful hard wuk; but de Lawd done sen He rabens, an He fiery chariots, an He pillows ob smoke, an now He done sen you Miss Hatty, like a bressed angel, fur to delibber us."

"He has indeed been very good to us," said the young lady, gently. "Now we must get this dear child home at once."

The carriage in which Miss Hatty was driving home from Richmond, when her curiosity was attracted by the strange scene in the little old cabin, was now brought to the door. Uncle Phin, feebly protesting that it was all too fine and too grand for a " wuffless ole niggah " like him, was made to take the front seat; while on the other sat Miss Harriet Dale, with ragged, tired, hungry, but intensely happy Arthur nestled close beside her.

The perplexing tumult of his feelings was such that, up to this time, he had not spoken a word; and even now he wondered if it were not all a beautiful dream, from which he would awake to find himself lying on the floor of the cabin. It seemed as though his own dear mother must have come back; that it was her loving arm now thrown protectingly about him, and he almost feared to speak, lest she might disappear, as she always did when he waked from dreaming of her. But the beautiful lady was talking to him and asking him questions.

She could not wait until they reached home to learn how these two had wandered from the faraway place in which she had met her " Prince Dusty," to this one. It was such a wonderful journey for them to have undertaken, that her impatience to know something of it could not be restrained. So she asked question after question, that Arthur and Uncle Phin answered to the best of their ability, until at length she knew enough of the principal events of their pilgrimage to make it seem marvellous that they should ever have accomplished it.

Among other things she learned of their experience in the runaway caboose of freight train No. 15, in the Alleghany Mountains, and this seemed to interest her more than all the rest.

Then she wanted to know if the book from which Arthur had been reading to Uncle Phin, and which he now carried clasped tightly in both hands, could be the same that she had given him so long ago, and how he had been able to keep it all this time.

"Of course it is," answered Arthur, "and of course I have kept it. It is the very most precious thing I own in the world; and nothing but beautiful things, just like its stories, have happened ever since you gave it to me. I had to let Rusty go to get us here; but I would never, never, have let my book go, not even if we had been starving."

Then Miss Hatty had to be told who Rusty was, and what a dear dog he was, and how hard it had been to part with him, and how Arthur hoped there would be some horses for him to hold at Dalecourt, or errands to be run, so that he could earn money enough to buy him back again.

It was too dark for them to see anything of the Park, once so carefully kept, but now neglected and overgrown, through which they drove for half a mile after turning in at the Dalecourt gateway; but Arthur felt a thrill of happiness when his cousin told him where they were. It seemed incredible that his long, weary journey, with all its hunger and cold and suffering, was past, and that he was really at the home he had so longed to reach. How beautiful it was to be welcomed so warmly and lovingly, when he had sometimes feared they might not even receive him at all.

At length the carriage stopped before a great rambling house, that had been very stately and handsome in bygone years; but which was now so dilapidated and shabby as to be but a forlorn relic of its former glory. However, it still contained much of comfort and good cheer; and, as the great front door was flung open, the warm glow of a huge log fire sprang out upon the cold darkness, and drove it back. It seemed to Arthur as though the very house offered him a welcome of light and warmth, and he loved it from that moment.

From the open doorway stepped an elderly gentleman, with iron-gray hair and mustache, and an erect military bearing, who called out:

"Welcome home, Niece Harriet! We've had lonely holidays without you; and right glad am I to have you back again."

"No more so than I am to be here, uncle!" exclaimed Miss Hatty, springing lightly from the carriage and heartily kissing the elderly gentleman, who was Colonel Arthur Dale, of Dalecourt, and Arthur's grandfather. "And, uncle, I've brought home a friend of yours, whom I picked up on the road. He is the very boy you were speaking of so recently, who saved your train, in the Alleghanies, from a collision."

"Eh! what's that?" cried Colonel Dale. "You have found that boy? How in the name of goodness—But bring him in! Bring him in where we can have a look at him. It's too cold to stand out here any longer."

So the young lady followed her uncle into the glowing hall, leading Arthur by the hand, while Uncle Phin hobbled after them. The boy's mind was filled with a whirl of conflicting emotions, as he stepped, for the first time, across the threshold of his mother's home, and gazed on the form of his nearest living relative. Had he tried to speak at that moment his feelings would have choked him; but he gave no outward sign of his mental condition, except by clasping more firmly the kind hand that led him forward.

When fairly within the circle of ruddy firelight, that filled the oak-panelled interior with its cheery glow, Colonel Dale turned for a look at the stranger whom his niece had so curiously discovered and brought home with her. As his glance fell on the ragged little figure at her side, the words that were upon his lips died away, a sudden pallor overspread his countenance, and he gazed in silence.

What did he see in that sweet face, now so thin and careworn? In its brave blue eyes? In the fair head of clustering ringlets? What was it that, for a moment, rendered him speechless and powerless to do aught save stare? It seemed to him that he saw a spirit.

"Who is he, Harriet?" he almost gasped, at length. "Where did you find him? He is the living image of my dead daughter?"

"He is that dead daughter's child, uncle. He is your own grandson Arthur, and my little 'Prince Dusty,'" was the answer.

The next instant the boy was clasped in a loving, forgiving, all-atoning embrace, and had found a place in his grandfather's heart, that he would never resign so long as life lasted.

CHAPTER XXVI.

COLONEL DALE OF DALECOURT.

IT is hardly possible to describe the joy that reigned in Dalecourt on that last night of the year. Colonel Dale and Miss Hatty, and Mrs. Allen Dale, her mother, all asked Arthur questions at once; and petted, and fed, and pitied, and praised him, until the poor, tired, happy little fellow, worn out with excitement, could no longer keep his eyes open, and was carried off to bed. Nor would it be possible to convey any idea of what a hero dear old Uncle Phin became in the eyes of the dusky assembly, who thronged the kitchen, to see him eat his much needed supper, and to hear of his marvellous adventures while bringing the "lil Marse" to his own home. All these things can be imagined a great deal better than they can be described. At the same time it does seem to be necessary to tell something about the Dales and Dalecourt, and how Colonel Dale's niece, Miss Harriet, happened to be the same beautiful lady who presented Arthur with an illustrated copy of Andersen's "Fairy Tales," in the oil region of Pennsylvania, some months before that happy New Year's Eve.

She was the only daughter of Colonel Dale's youngest brother Allen, and was therefore own cousin to Arthur's mother. At the death of her father, who left them penniless, she and her mother went to Dalecourt to live, and to keep house for her lonely uncle.

One of the very dearest of Miss Hatty's school friends lived in the oil region of Pennsylvania, and during the previous summer she paid this friend a visit. It was at the conclusion of this visit, and while driving from her friend's house to the distant railway station, that she encountered Arthur and little Cynthia, just as their search for adventures had led them into trouble.

With her first glance at the boy's face she was struck by a certain familiar expression in it, and when he told her his name she wondered if he might not be her little cousin whom she had never seen.

She was not quite sure of the Dustin part of his name, as it was never allowed to be mentioned at Dalecourt, so she decided to wait until she could make further inquiries before claiming the relationship.

As she had barely time to reach the railway station and catch her train, she was not able to pursue these inquiries just then. She, however, bade the coachman find out what he could about the Dustins, and also wrote to her friend for what information she could obtain concerning the child, in whom she had become so greatly interested. From her mother she learned that Dustin was the name of the young Northerner whom her cousin Virginia had married; and when she received an answer to her letter, it assured her that she had discovered, in that far-away region, her uncle's only grandson.

Now came what she feared would prove the most difficult part of her task. Colonel Dale had forbidden the name of Dustin to be mentioned in his house, nor had Miss Hatty ever heard him speak as though aware that he had a grandson living. She at first tried to approach the subject cautiously, but finding that she was liable to be misunderstood, she at length told her uncle frankly all that she knew and suspected. To her great surprise he listened to her willingly and with an eager interest.

Colonel Arthur Dale had been a very selfish man, though he called his selfishness "family pride." He had also been a very self-willed one, though this he would have said indicated strength of character.

Of late years, however, both of these faults had been dealt heavy blows. The losing of his beautiful daughter Virginia was the first blow. Then his wife died, and then the war came. It left him a poor man, with a large but unproductive estate on his hands, and no opportunity, that he could discover, for going into business and retrieving his shattered fortunes.

Instead of hardening his nature, these trials softened it. His pride was broken. He no longer thought of himself alone. His stubbornness disappeared and he longed for human love and sympathy. His once princely estate was now so encumbered by mortgages that they promised soon completely to overwhelm it. It spite of its owner's efforts to keep the place in order, it showed evidences of decay and ruin in every direction. Many of the old family servants still clung to Dalecourt, and the Colonel was too kind-hearted to turn them away. Thus there was always a large number of mouths to feed, and each year brought less to feed them with.

Of late the lonely man had thought much of his dead daughter, and wondered if her son, the grandson whose existence he had never openly acknowledged, was still alive, and what sort of a boy he was. Thus, when his niece began to speak to him on this very subject, he proved an eager listener to all that she had to say.

"He is one of the very dearest, sweetest, and bravest little fellows I ever saw," she cried impulsively. "When I met him he was making believe to be a prince, and was defending a child, younger than himself, from what he thought was the savage attack of a big dog. He was so covered with dust when I picked him up out of the road, that I called him 'Prince Dusty,' and the title of 'Prince' seems somehow exactly to suit him. Although he was ragged and barefooted, he was every inch a little gentleman, and the last I saw of him he was lifting his tattered straw hat to me, as I drove away."

The result of this conversation, and of several

similar ones that followed it, was that, toward the end of October, Colonel Dale set out for the oil region of Pennsylvania, determined to bring his dead daughter's child home with him, and thereafter to treat him as his own son.

He had, by this time, so set his heart upon having the boy to love and to care for, and had centred so many plans for the future about him, that to learn, from the Dustins, of Arthur's absolute and mysterious disappearance, was a grievous disappointment, for which he was not prepared. He could not believe that the boy was not still in that vicinity, and insisted that a search should be made for him throughout all the surrounding country, though the runaways had been gone for nearly a month.

Colonel Dale read and re-read the rudely pencilled note that Arthur had left for Cynthia, and asked to be allowed to keep it: but the child would not give it up. It was her most treasured possession, and though he bribed her with money, and candy, and toys, she could not be induced to part with it.

Brace Barlow, the only person who knew how and in what direction Arthur and Uncle Phin had gone, was in a distant part of the oil region, so that he heard nothing of Colonel Dale's arrival, nor of the eager search for the little fellow who used to call him "dear giant."

Arthur's grandfather even visited the farm that had belonged to his unacknowledged son-in-law, Richard Dustin, with the faint hope that his grandson might have sought shelter there.

Finally, after obtaining John Dustin's promise to telegraph the first bit of information that he should gain concerning the missing boy, and also to relinquish all claims upon him in favor of the grandfather, the disappointed man turned his face homeward. He was not only disappointed at the unexpected result of his journey; but he was as heavy-hearted as though death had robbed him of some loved one, and he were now on his way to bear the sad tidings to those who waited at home.

It was such thoughts as these that drove sleep from his eyes, while the Keystone express, on which he was a passenger, climbed the western slope of the Alleghanies, and barely escaped destruction from the runaway caboose of a freight train, through the prompt action of a boy. If the sleepless man could only have known that this boy was his own grandson, how quickly would his sorrow have been changed to joy and pride. As it was, he was filled with admiration for the brave lad, merely from listening to the sleeping-car porter's imperfect account of the affair, and wished he might have seen and known him.

When he reached home he related this incident to his niece and her mother as the most thrilling of his trip, and again regretted that he had not made the acquaintance of its hero.

Now, the fact that his grandson and this young hero were one and the same boy, and that this boy had voluntarily sought a home under his roof, was a continual source of joy and pride to Colonel Dale, that he was at no pains to conceal.

Becomingly dressed, well cared for, and, above all, surrounded by an atmosphere of love and gentleness, "Prince Dusty" was now such a handsome, merry little fellow, that he not only completely won the hearts of his grandfather and the Dalecourt household, but of every one who came in contact with him.

Now, more bitterly than ever, did Colonel Dale regret his lost fortune, and shrink from the ruin that, staring him in the face, could not much longer be averted. The financial difficulties of the family had not been kept from Arthur, for he was wise beyond his years, and his grandfather thought it best that he should know exactly how matters stood with them. It was a great grief to the boy to see his grandpapa and his Cousin Hatty, both of whom he had learned to love dearly, so troubled; and, in his wise young way, he pondered deeply over the situation.

At last, one evening as he was bidding them all good-night, he said: "Grandpapa, I think I have almost thought of a way for us to get a great deal of money."

"Have you, my boy?" said the colonel. "That's good; what is it?"

"Well I have n't quite thought it all out yet; but I will finish thinking and tell you what it is in the morning," replied the boy, smiling brightly down upon his grandfather, as he bounded up the broad stairway.

CHAPTER XXVII.

A "GENUINE CHUMP."

IT seemed so absurd that a twelve-year-old boy should be considering plans for raising the large sum of money necessary to help Colonel Dale out of his difficulties, that, after Arthur had gone to bed, those who were left downstairs found considerable amusement in wondering what his scheme could be.

His grandfather said it would probably be a proposition to form an errand-boy trust; while Mrs. Dale thought it would only prove to be some absurd idea concerning railroad life, that the boy had picked up during his recent travels. Miss Harriet, however, said that her "Prince Dusty" was wiser than they imagined, and she did not believe he ever spoke seriously, upon any subject, without knowing pretty well what he was saying. So, by talking the matter over, they became greatly interested, and quite curious to hear what Arthur would have to say the next morning.

When they began to question him at breakfast time he gravely answered that he had heard his papa say that the breakfast-table was not the proper place to discuss business affairs. The seriousness with which this speech was uttered, caused a general smile, and as Colonel Dale had been heard to make the very same remark, no objections could be raised against it.

After breakfast the little fellow invited his grandfather to accompany him into the library, where he proceeded to unfold his plan. It was nothing more nor less than that they should go back to Pennsylvania, and sink a well, for oil, on the farm that his father had left him.

For a moment Colonel Dale looked at the boy to see if he were in earnest, and then burst into a hearty laugh. "Why, Arthur!" he said at length, "whatever put such an idea into your head? I don't know the first thing about oil wells, and I am afraid that, wise as you are, you don't know much more than I do."

"That's just it, sir!" replied the boy, eagerly. "And it is because both of us are 'chumps' that we'll be certain to strike oil. Brace Barlow always said so. You see, a 'chump' is somebody who does n't know any more about oil, or where to find it, than we do. What Brace Barlow says is, that while those who know all about the business often strike 'dusters,' a 'genuine chump' always has luck with his first well. Now, you are a 'genuine chump,' you know. I 'm afraid I am not quite genuine, because Brace Barlow has told me so much about the business, and because I helped him shoot a well. But, I think you must be genuine enough for both of us. It 's a perfectly splendid way to make money, unless you strike a 'duster,' but only 'sharps' do that."

"What do you mean by 'dusters' and 'sharps'? They sound exceedingly like slang words," said Colonel Dale, smiling.

"Oh, no, indeed, they are not!" cried Arthur. "Brace Barlow uses them, and so does Uncle John. A 'duster' is a dry well—one that does n't have any oil, you know; and a 'sharp' is one who understands all about the oil business. He is just the most different kind of a man from a 'chump,' and is nearly always too wise to make money."

"But, my boy, your farm is not even in the oil region; so what makes you fancy that we could strike oil by sinking a well on it?" asked Colonel Dale.

"Because I know two secrets about it," answered the boy, mysteriously. "One day when papa and I were walking in the back wood-lot, we smelled gas, and by and by we found a tiny place in the rocks where it came out. Papa lighted it, and it burned beautifully. Then he put it out, and told me always to remember that place, but not to say anything about it to anybody until the proper time came. After that papa studied a great deal about oil, and he found out that our farm was on the forty-five degree line, and said he was quite sure that oil would some day be found on it.

"So, while he did n't tell anybody but me about it, he made Uncle John promise never to sell the farm. I have thought several times, when I needed money, that I would go back to my farm and get some oil to sell; but then it has always come some other way, so I have n't had to touch it. Then I thought I would save it, until I was ready to be a railroad man, and wanted to build a railroad of my own. Now I have decided that I would rather you should have it than to do anything else in the world with it, and then you can make Dalecourt beautiful again, and we can always live here and be happy."

Although at the time Colonel Dale made light of his little grandson's plans for acquiring wealth, this curious conversation set him to thinking, and to looking up all the information concerning oil that he could obtain. The more he considered the scheme, the more favorably he was impressed with it, and the more inclined he was to attempt it.

Mrs. Allen Dale thought it was all nonsense; but Miss Harriet was delighted with it, and begged her uncle to undertake it. "Just think!" she exclaimed, "how fine it would be, if our little 'Prince Dusty' should turn out to be a little oil Prince. Would n't it be splendid?"

At length, when the winter had passed, and the Virginia forests were putting on their delicate spring robes of leaves and blossoms, Colonel Dale decided to make the venture, and to sink a "wild-cat" well on the Pennsylvania farm belonging to his grandson, with the hope of finding oil.

It was a curious thing for a staid and elderly Virginia planter to undertake; and, but for the desperate state of his fortunes, it is doubtful if he would have considered the plan for a moment. As it was, he mortgaged Dalecourt for the very last cent that could possibly be raised on it, and, with the few thousand dollars thus obtained, started for Pennsylvania.

Arthur and Miss Harriet accompanied him; the former, as a matter of course, because, as he said, he was to be his grandpapa's partner in this new business. The latter went to keep house for them while the well was being sunk, and to continue Arthur's education, which she had undertaken when he first came to Dalecourt. Mrs. Dale was to remain in charge of the beautiful old place, which might so soon pass into the hands of strangers, and Uncle Phin was also left behind to fill the responsible position of head gardener.

On the morning that the little party set forth on the journey that, to them, promised as much of glorious success or disastrous failure as did ever an ancient voyage of discovery or exploration, Arthur was enthusiastic over their undertaking, and confident of its complete success. Miss Harriet was smiling and hopeful. Colonel Dale was serious, and his face wore an air of quiet determination; while Mrs. Allen Dale was tearful and doubtful. She bade them good-bye as though she never expected to see them again; and, when they were gone, she gazed as sadly about her, as though the last hope of Dalecourt had departed with them.

The journey was a rapid and pleasant one, occupying but two days and one night, which was in striking contrast to the three months spent by Arthur and Uncle Phin in traversing the same distance.

Arthur did not manifest much interest in Washington, as they passed through it. He had suffered too much there to care to renew his associations with the place. He only looked eagerly from the car window at all the dogs that were to be seen, with the faint hope that one of them might be his dear Rusty.

At Harrisburg he tried to point out to his companions Conductor Tobin's cottage; and, from there to Pittsburgh, he felt almost certain that every freight train they passed must be No. 15, and that on each he recognized Brakeman Joe. He was greatly disappointed that they did not have time to go and see Aunt Charity; for he gratefully remembered all those who had been kind to him in the time of his need, and would gladly have renewed their acquaintance.

CHAPTER XXVIII.

A FEW FACTS CONCERNING PETROLEUM.

AS they approached the oil region, and began to see the tall derricks, looking like windmill towers, crowning the hilltops, their conversation naturally turned upon the subject of oil and its production. Arthur related stories from Brace Barlow's experience; while Colonel Dale, who, from weeks of reading, was now as well informed on on all matters pertaining to oil as one can be from books alone, gave them bits of information concerning its early use and history.

One of Arthur's stories described the fearfully narrow escape his "dear giant" once had from a runaway team. He was driving along a lonely road that ran in the bottom of a narrow valley, and had sixty quarts of nitro-glycerine snugly stowed under the seat of his buggy. Suddenly he saw a runaway team attached to a heavy lumber wagon, dashing at a mad gallop down the road, directly toward him. There was barely time to turn his own horses into the ditch at one side, and thus leave a narrow space through which the runaways might have passed in safety, if they had so chosen.

Instead of doing this, they too headed for the ditch, and plunged into it, just in front of the glycerine buggy. There they fell over each other, broke the pole, upset their wagon, and became so entangled in the wreck that they were incapable of further mischief. All this took place within ten feet of where Brace Barlow sat, on top of his load of nitroglycerine, as steadily as though he did not expect, with each instant, to be blown into a million fragments, and hurled into eternity.

Then Colonel Dale explained what torpedoes are, and why they are used; and Miss Hatty said she hoped their well would have to be shot, so that she might witness the operation. Seeing that his companions were interested in the subject, the Colonel continued to talk of it. He said:

"Although we, naturally, know and hear more about the oil fields of Pennsylvania than any other, petroleum is also found in a dozen or more of our own States and territories, as well as in many other countries of the world. 'In Pennsylvania it exists in a narrow territory, lying about fifty miles west of the Alleghany Mountains; and, as the oil-bearing belt extends in a general northeast and southwest direction, it is spoken of as lying on a forty-five-degree line."

"Just as our farm does," said Arthur.

"Exactly," said his grandfather, "and I only hope it may not lie over one of the many barren places that exist on that line."

"In this part of the country," he continued, "the drilling of wells and the handling of oil have been reduced to a state of perfection and simplicity unknown elsewhere. Consequently, Pennsylvania well drillers, with their tools, are in demand in many foreign oil fields, and may be found, commanding large salaries, in Russia, Japan, China, New Zealand, Canada, the various countries of Western South America, in several of the West Indian islands, and elsewhere.

"In China immense oil fields exist, in which wells, drilled centuries ago, are still in use. Natural gas has also been used in that country for hundreds, and perhaps thousands, of years. It is conveyed from the wells through bamboo pipes tipped with rude clay burners.

"Petroleum has also been known and used in Burmah for an unknown length of time, both for light and fuel. Into a shallow oil well of that country an iron bucket is lowered by means of a rope, passing over a wooden cylinder. When the bucket is full, two men take hold of the other end of the rope, and, by running down an inclined plane as long as the well is deep, draw it to the surface."

"What a stupid way," said Miss Hatty.

"Havana, Cuba," continued Colonel Dale, "was originally named 'Carine,' for it was the place where the early voyagers to the new world careened their vessels and made their seams water-tight with the natural pitch, or solidified petroleum, that oozed in abundance from the rocks near the shores of the harbor. Oil springs are very numerous in Cuba, as they are in many others of the West Indian islands."

"Would n't it be good if we could find a flowing oil spring on our farm?" said Arthur, his eyes glistening at the prospect.

"It would certainly be very pleasant," replied his grandfather. "And, speaking of flowing springs, the most wonderful flow of petroleum ever seen in any country, occurred in 1862 in the town of Enniskillen, in the western part of the Canadian Province of Ontario, along the borders of a stream called Black Creek. At that time there was so little demand for oil that it was only bringing ten cents a barrel, though three years later it was worth ten dollars a barrel in gold.

"The first well in that region was drilled early in the year; and, at the depth of only one hundred feet, it entered an immense reservoir of petroleum. Although oil was of so little value at that time, the reckless settlers of the country seemed possessed of a rage for drilling wells, apparently merely for the pleasure of seeing it flow from them. Some of these rudely drilled wells spouted forth thousands of barrels of oil in a day, and one of them is computed to have flowed at the rate of 10,000 barrels in twenty-four hours. All these fountains and rivers of oil were allowed to run absolutely to waste. The waters of Black Creek were covered by it to a depth of six inches, and it formed a film over the entire surface of Lake Erie.

"At length this vast quantity of oil was set on fire by some mischievous person, who wished to see what the effect would be. For days Black Creek was a torrent of raging flames, that leaped and roared with inconceivable fury and grandeur. It was such a sight as the world never had seen, and probably never will see again; while the Canadians were so thoroughly satisfied with their experiment that they have had no desire to repeat it since.

"It is estimated that, during the spring and summer of 1862, no less than five millions of barrels of oil ran to waste down the channel of Black Creek. Three years later that amount of oil would have been worth, in the United States, a hundred million of dollars."

"My!" exclaimed Arthur, drawing a long breath. "I don't believe I should know what to do with so much money as that."

"I am afraid you would n't, dear," laughed Miss Hatty. "I know that I for one would not dare assume the responsibility of taking care of, and spending, such an enormous sum. Why, the man who has one hundredth part of that, or one million, has more money than many princes, and is wealthy beyond the average conception; while he who has but a thousandth part of it, or one hundred thousand dollars, is still a rich man."

Although Arthur hardly comprehended these figures, they interested him, and he now asked: "How many barrels of oil will we have to get out of our well, grandpapa, to give us as much money as we need?"

"That is rather a hard question to answer," laughed Colonel Dale; "for, as a general thing, the more money people have, the more they think they need. However, always supposing that it is not a 'duster,' as you have taught me to call a dry hole, if our well yields twenty-five barrels a day I shall be pleased. If it should yield fifty barrels I should be perfectly satisfied; while with a daily yield of one hundred barrels, I should be amazed and delighted. In that case you might well be called a 'little oil Prince'; for, with oil at three dollars per barrel, your income would be at the rate of a hundred thousand dollars a year."

"But suppose it should yield more than a hundred barrels a day?" persisted Arthur. "How would you feel then?"

"I am sure I do not know," laughed his grandfather, "for I cannot conceive of such a thing as happening. I expect I should feel something as Mr. Kier of Pittsburgh did in 1860, when the oil that he had been getting at the rate of two or three barrels a day from his salt wells, and selling as a medicine for fifty cents a half pint, was suddenly produced in such quantities that the price fell to about ten cents per barrel. So, if our well should flow too freely, I should be afraid that its product would become a drug on the market."

"Just what Mr. Kier's had been, but ceased to be," laughed Miss Hatty.

"What?" asked Arthur, innocently.

"Why, a drug on the market. Did n't uncle say that it was formerly sold as a medicine?"

"Oh, yes," said Arthur, soberly, "I see."

Just then Miss Hatty, who was very fond of figs, invested ten cents in a small box of "fig tablets," as the train-boy called them. She and Arthur at once began to eat them with evident relish, but Colonel Dale refused the proffered box.

"What do you suppose you are eating?" he asked, smiling.

"Why, figs of course," answered Miss Hatty.

"Do you call that a fig leaf?" asked her uncle, pointing to one, cut from green paper, that lay on top of the box.

"No, certainly not. That is only an imitation leaf," was the answer.

"Well, it is just as much a real leaf as those are real figs."

"Why, grandpapa, they have seeds in them!" exclaimed Arthur, as though that was proof positive that they must be real figs.

"To be sure they have," laughed Colonel Dale. "The imitation would not be a good one if the seeds were left out. In spite of their seeds, those figs are made of petroleum; or rather of paraffine, which is one of the important products of petroleum. Not long ago I came across a list of over two hundred articles of commerce that are manufactured directly from this wonderful oil. Among them were these very 'fig tablets.' Other things made from paraffine are chewing-gum, jujube paste, gum-drops, some jellies and jams, icing for cakes, etc. The list also contained the names of all our most brilliant dyes, which are produced from the very lowest residuum of petroleum tar, and several drugs, among which was a powerful anæsthetic."

"Well," said Miss Hatty, "I am glad I am not so wise as some people. It is very foolish to know too much; for it takes half the pleasure out of life. Now I am sure I don't care to eat any more of these kerosene figs, even if they have got seeds in them; and yet a minute ago I thought them quite good."

"Seems to me," said practical little Arthur, "that it is more foolish not to eat a thing that tastes good, if it won't do you any harm, no matter what it is made of, than it is to be wise."

"And it seems to me," said Colonel Dale, "that we had better be collecting our things and preparing to leave the train; for here is the station at which we are to get off."

CHAPTER XXIX.

LOCATING AN OIL WELL.

IT was a comfortable, low-roofed, stone farm-house, at which the stage deposited our travellers, after a pleasant drive from the railway station. To Arthur it seemed very much like a home, so filled was it with memories of his dear father. As Colonel Dale had notified the neighbor, who had it in charge, of their coming, everything was in readiness for them. The house had been aired and swept, its plain but serviceable furniture dusted and cleaned, lights were burning in all the lower rooms, and supper was nearly ready.

Miss Hatty, who had never been there before, was charmed with the place, and hoped that if they lost Dalecourt they could make their home here in "Prince Dusty's" castle.

They did not tell anybody why they came into

that out-of-the-way part of the world, and many were the discussions throughout the scattered neighborhood as to the object of their visit. At length old Deacon Thackby thought he had discovered the secret and he announced the fact, with a wise look on his shrewd face, as he and several others stood on the church steps after a Friday evening meeting.

"I figgered out yesterday," he said, "why them Dales come here and settled down like they was going to stay."

"I thought maybe from the way I see him peering round that p'raps he was perspecting fer ile," piped a thin voice at the Deacon's elbow.

"Ile!" snorted the Deacon, contemptuously. "You've got ile on the brain, brother Moss. Ef thar was any ile raound here would n't some of us that was borned and brung up in the place have diskivered it long ago? Do you suppose a stranger, who I reckin never seed a drap of crude in his life, is a comin to tell us what we never knowed about our own kentry, nor what our fathers never knowed, nor what nobody never will know?

"Well——" said the thin voice.

"Well!" interrupted the Deacon. "There's no use talking. It may be ile that has brung 'em here; but it's paint ile, an not petroleum. That young woman is one of them artiss's that you hear so much about nowadays, an she's here to do some paintin. The boy wanted to come naturally 'cause it was his home, an the old Cunnel he come to look after 'em. That's all thar is about it."

"What makes you think the young lady is an artist, Deacon?" asked another of the group.

"I don't think, I know," replied Deacon Thackby, decidedly, "an how I know is 'cause I seen her at it, and 'cause she's cranky and pernicketly like they all is. Why, last Wednesday she come down to my old red mill an did a drawring of it, an called it a beautiful color subjec, an said she was comin down agin yesterday afternoon to do it in iles. Well, you know how drefful shabby-looking the old place was, all kinder cluttered up, an the paint wore off in patches, an them vines hiding the best half of it.

"It seemed too bad to have her wastin her time on sich as it was, an I did n't want folks to look at her picter, when it was done, an say how shifless I was nohow. So I got the boys out by the break o' day, an we put in some good solid work on that mill agin the time she got thar. We tore down all them pesky vines an burned them up, an cut away the bushes so as to make a good airy clearin all raound. Then we turned to an giv the hull outside a fust-class coat of whitewash, from ruff to suller, an made it look fine.

"We had n't more 'n finished when she come along with all her fixins, ready to do it up in iles; but when I went out to show her what we 'd done she did n't seem a mite grateful. She jest looked disappointed an miserable an said 'Oh, Deacon, how could ye?'

"Then she went off, like she felt real bad, an awhile afterwards I see her settin on the big rock in my hill pasture, wastin all her paints on one of them common pink an white apple-trees, such as you might see most any day bout this time o' year. Oh, yes, she 's a artiss, an cranky like they all is."

In the meantime Colonel Dale was quietly, but actively, making preparations to sink a well, in search of the wealth of oil that he hoped lay hidden beneath the Dustin farm. On the very first morning after they reached there he and Miss Hatty and Arthur visited the place in the back wood-lot where Mr. Dustin and his son had discovered the tiny gas jet issuing from the rocks. Arthur readily found it again, and again the application of a lighted match gave proof that it was genuine gas and would burn.

Then the Colonel said he would leave the location of the well to his little partner, and asked him to point out the place where he wished the derrick to stand.

The boy walked hesitatingly around the gas jet for a minute, and then, returning to where the others stood, said :

"Don't you think, grandpapa, that Cousin Hatty 'd better be the one to say where it shall stand? You see I know so much about oil, and you have got so wise lately, that I am afraid we are not quite such 'chumps' as we ought to be; but Cousin Hatty is a real genuine, and does n't know anything at all. About oil, I mean!" he added quickly, blushing furiously. "Of course she knows everything else, and that 's what makes her the very best kind of a 'chump.'"

"Something like—

> "'The pork-pie man's beautiful daughter
> Who rarely knew what she had orter ;
> And in quenching a fire,
> Once sought to rise higher,
> Using ile, instead of cold water,'"

laughed Miss Hatty. "However, I will consent to act as the 'chump' of this party for the sake of the common good, and I decide that the well shall be sunk on this very spot." Here the young lady thrust a bit of stick into the ground where she was standing. It was about a hundred feet from the little gas jet, on the side nearest the house, and Miss Hatty afterwards acknowledged that she selected it because it was visible from her window, and she wanted to be able to see the derrick when it was built.

The spot where that bit of stick stood in the ground instantly acquired a new interest. It almost seemed as though they could see the tall derrick that was to rise there, and hear the steady thud of the drill as it cut its way down through earth and rock to the oil-bed. The very air seemed to be filled with the odor of petroleum ; but perhaps it was only a whiff of the gas driven towards them by a puff of wind. At any rate, they felt that a beginning had been made now that the site of the well was decided upon, and were more than ever anxious to have the work go speedily forward.

Soon afterwards Colonel Dale visited the old oil region, some twenty miles away, in which Mr. John Dustin lived, to purchase the necessary supplies for his well, and to engage experienced men to come and drill it. It was while he was thus absent that Deacon Thackby persuaded the neighborhood that the Dales were only there because Miss Hatty was an "artiss."

The neighborhood was indeed astonished when it discovered one day that several loads of lumber had been hauled from the railway station to the Dustin farm, and that a "rig-builder" was at work with his men erecting a derrick in the back wood-lot.

"What in the name of common-sense!" ejaculated Deacon Thackby, when he first heard of what was going on.

"Did n't I tell ye I thought they was perspecting round fer ile?" piped brother Moss' thin voice.

"But thar ain't no ile within twenty mile of here" cried Deacon Thackby. "The man must be a born natural to come wild-catting down here, and I'm jest a going to tell him so."

And the Deacon did tell Colonel Dale how foolishly he was, wasting his money, and how perfectly useless it was to drill for oil in that part of the country, where, if there was any, it would have been discovered long ago.

"Has anybody tried sinking a well in this vicinity?" asked Colonel Dale.

"Yes, thar was Sile Pettis put one down 'bout a year ago; but it did n't mount to nothing. Thar warn't no ile into it."

"How deep did he sink it?" inquired the Colonel, with interest.

"Well, not more than four hundred foot or so," admitted the Deacon, reluctantly.

"And the 'third sand,' which is the only one in this region that pays—or at least so I am told," remarked the Colonel, "is hardly ever struck at a less depth than one thousand feet. Is Mr. Sile Pettis' unproductive well the only thing that makes you think there is no oil about here, Deacon?"

"Thar ain't no surface indications, like thar should be if the ile was right down under us."

"That is something we must provide for at once," laughed Arthur's grandfather. "I realize that we must have them, Deacon, and just as soon as I get this well down a thousand feet I will try and show you some of the finest surface indications in the country."

CHAPTER XXX.

THE DALE-DUSTIN MYSTERY.

ALTHOUGH Colonel Dale talked thus bravely and cheerfully, he could not drive away a heavy, sinking feeling from his heart, nor prevent the furrows in his face from growing deeper and deeper, as he thought of how much depended upon the result of this experiment that everybody about him said was such a foolish waste of both time and money.

Still the work was pushed steadily forward. The graceful derrick was run rapidly up to a height of sixty feet, and a strong iron pulley wheel was suspended from its crown. On the derrick floor, at one side, the great bull wheels, about the shaft of which the drill rope was to be wound, were placed in position. On the opposite side was set the solid samson post that was to support the equally solid walking beam. The former was a section of the squared trunk of an oak tree, let deep into the ground; while the walking beam was a long and very strong oaken timber, nicely balanced so that it would work readily up and down. To the end of the walking beam, that reached into the middle of the derrick, were to be attached the heavy drills; while the other end was connected with the ten-horse-power engine that stood in a rough shed but a short distance from the derrick.

Still beyond this, in the open air, was a rusty boiler, with a pipe discharging into its open furnace door. This pipe led from a small tank that was filled by the jet of natural gas, discovered by Arthur and his father; and natural gas was to be the only fuel used in drilling and operating the Dale-Dustin well.

At length, after a month of hard work and vexatious delays, the "rig-builders" finished their labors, and the well drillers came in their place. To Arthur's great joy, they were headed by his "dear giant," Brace Barlow, who, having heard that his little friend was interested in a new oil well, applied for and obtained the contract for drilling it. "And Arthur, lad," he said, after the first warmth of their greeting was over, "if this well proves a 'duster,' it won't be because it is n't drilled fair enough, or deep enough. I 'll keep the temper screw turning, and the drill going, till we strike something to stop it, if it 's only an order to quit, or the bottom of the appropriation."

Brace Barlow brought with him a delightful surprise for Arthur in the person of his Cousin Cynthia, who, upon Miss Hatty's invitation, came to make a visit at Dustin farm. The two children enjoyed each other so thoroughly that it was a pleasure to see them together. Arthur had so much to tell and Cynthia so much to hear concerning his wonderful journey to Dalecourt, and they had so many plans to make for the future, that the days were not half long enough for them. In the evenings, when the day's work was done, Arthur generally sat with Brace Barlow, listening to his tales of adventure in the oil region, or relating incidents of the recent journey, in which Brace was fully as much interested as Cynthia.

Thus the boy discovered how the mysterious five-dollar bill came to be in his precious book, and Brace learned of what service it had been to them.

Day after day the powerful drills worked steadily downward through hard and soft rock, sometimes descending only six or eight feet in twenty-four hours, but generally cutting through twenty or thirty feet of material in a day. The first and second sandstones or "sands" were passed, and at length the drill was down a thousand feet. At this depth it had not yet reached the third, or oil-bearing, sandstone. Occasional puffs of gas came up through the casing of iron pipe that was driven down as fast as a hole was cut to receive it; but there was no sign of oil.

The work had now been prosecuted for two months, and with the passage of time, and the rapid melting away of the few remaining dollars of his fortune, Colonel Dale's face grew more furrowed and careworn, and, though he still tried to maintain a brave front, it was evident that anxiety was telling heavily upon him.

As the opening of a new district has a very decided effect on the oil market, all brokers who deal in oil or oil stocks are, of course, anxious to secure the earliest information concerning the prospects of the first well sunk in it. If this proves to be a dry-hole, and the district is accordingly believed to be barren, the price of oil remains firm, with a tendency to go up. If, on the other hand, the new well happens to be a "gusher," the price of oil immediately drops. In either case those who receive the earliest reliable information are able to make their purchases or sales of oil accordingly and reap large profits.

In order to obtain this information some of the leading brokers and oil companies employ a class of men called "scouts," whose duty it is to find out all about new wells, especially those drilled in districts hitherto unworked, and to report upon their progress and prospects. These scouts are always bright young fellows, thoroughly posted in all details of the oil business; and it is almost impossible to keep the condition of any well a secret from them, even though the owners undertake to do so.

Now Colonel Dale had determined to reap, for Arthur's sake, whatever benefits were to be gained from an early knowledge of the prospects of the Dale-Dustin well. For this purpose he had engaged the services of a broker in Oil City, whom he had undertaken to furnish with the very earliest information regarding it. As the drill neared the depth at which it was expected to enter the oil-bearing rock, a number of scouts began to appear on the scene of operations and to visit the well every day. On the approach of the critical hour that was to decide the fate of the experiment, these visitors were politely but firmly requested to keep off the premises, while the derricks and tanks were boarded up, so that they might not be able to witness the inside operations from a distance. The drillers were bound to secrecy regarding the progress of their work, and a guard was stationed about the well, with orders not to allow any stranger to approach the derrick. Thus the Dale-Dustin well became a "mystery," and the scouts were put to their wits' end to discover its condition.

They formed a camp among the thick hemlocks, back of the Dustin farm, and at the nearest point to the well they could reach. Here one or more of their number remained on watch night and day, with fleet horses beside them, ready to bear them to the nearest telegraph station with the first bit of information they should obtain. From this camp a powerful field glass was always directed toward the new derrick, the strokes of the walking-beam were counted, and every movement of those who came out of, or went into, the boarded structure was closely watched.

During the darkness of night the scouts crept closer, and, with many a narrow escape from the guards, who constantly patrolled the premises, watched and listened for any chance bit of news that might thus be gleaned.

At last their patience and perseverance were rewarded, and they gained the very information for which they had striven so long. A scout, who had lain concealed in a clump of low bushes beside the derrick, during the long hours of a dark, stormy night, overheard a remark not intended for his ears. It furnished a key to the situation; and, slipping away, still unobserved, to where his horse was fastened, he galloped rapidly off in the direction of the village.

In the several oil exchanges of the country, the principal item of news the next morning was that the Dale-Dustin mystery well had proved a dry hole; and many were the jokes made concerning the Dustin "duster."

CHAPTER XXXI.

A BITTER DISAPPOINTMENT.

THE Dale-Dustin well was a dry hole. It contained a little gas and plenty of salt water; but not a drop of oil flowed from it, though, as Brace Barlow said, the material through which the drill had finally pierced, at a depth of twelve hundred feet, was as likely looking oil sand as one would wish to see. The boss driller was greatly puzzled to account for the present state of affairs, though he was not inclined to talk much about it. He had so often and so confidently predicted that this well was not only going to strike oil, but to prove a "gusher," that he now had nothing to say.

He spent the greater part of the morning in wandering moodily about the place, occasionally entering the derrick, and casting reproachful glances at the idle drills, as though they were in some way responsible for having opened such a useless hole in the ground. Then he would pick up a handful of sand, from a little pile on the derrick floor, where the sand-pump, that brought it from the very bottom of the well, had deposited it. He would smell of this sand, and taste it, and rub it slowly between his fingers. Then, with a perplexed shake of his head, the "dear giant" would throw it away, and again set forth on his melancholy wanderings about the place. He had discharged and paid off his men that morning; so now he was left entirely alone with his thoughts. At length, about noon, he disappeared, and nobody knew what had become of him.

The night before, his tour of duty, or "tower," as the oil men say, began at midnight, when he took charge of the drilling, with one assistant. They found that the tools had entered the third sand, in which it had been expected to strike oil, and were rapidly cutting their way through it. The layer of sandstone at this point was unusually thick, and it was not until nearly daylight that the drill penetrated beyond it.

With each drop of the tools, the anxious watchers at the surface expected a rush of oil; and each time the sand-pump was let down, its return was eagerly awaited, and its contents were carefully examined. There were, to be sure, traces of oil; but that was all.

All night long, Colonel Dale sat in the derrick, hardly speaking or moving, except when he stepped forward to study the contents of the sand-pump. It was a night of nights to him. His fortunes, and those of the dear ones dependent upon him, were to be decided by the result of those few hours' labor.

A derrick lamp cast an uncertain light over the scene, and threw long wavering shadows across the floor. Brace Barlow worked the temper screw, and turned the drill after each stroke, so as to insure its cutting a perfectly round hole. His assistant labored at the little, glowing forge in one corner. Here he heated the extra drills, and, on the anvil beside him, beat their blunted points into sharp, cutting edges with a heavy hammer.

There was a steady clangor of noise within the boarded structure; while outside the wind howled dismally. Conversation would have been difficult; and, under the circumstances, there was nothing that any of the three men cared to say. Colonel Dale's face grew whiter and whiter, as the slow hours passed, and the monotonous working of the tools produced no result. His eyes were fixed upon the great drill rope, as it moved steadily up and down, but he did not see it. He saw his dearly loved grandson, and his niece, thrown on the charity of the world. He saw Dalecourt, his once beautiful home, and the home of his fathers, passing from him, and occupied by strangers. He saw himself ruined and helpless, pointed at by men as an old fool, who had persisted in squandering his money on a reckless adventure that everybody told him would only result in failure.

He hardly knew when the monotonous throb of the machinery ceased; but, in the stillness that followed, he heard the tones of Brace Barlow's voice, something like those of a judgment. Standing respectfully and pityingly before him, the young man said :

"I hate to tell you, Colonel; but it's no use drilling any further. We've gone clean through the sand without a show. I don't understand it, but it's so all the same, and it would be foolish to spend any more money on such a 'duster' as this hole has proved."

"Very well, Mr. Barlow," replied Colonel Dale, speaking calmly and without a trace of emotion, "pay off the men and discharge them. I am going to the house for a nap. Please see that I am not disturbed or awakened." Then the stricken man, with the merciless hand of ruin clutching at his throat, walked slowly away from the scene of his high hopes and bitter disappointment.

In the stillness that followed the stopping of the machinery, Brace Barlow's words had been plainly heard by the oil scout, who crouched, wet, cold, and well-nigh exhausted, in his hiding-place close beside the derrick. It was what he had waited for; and, an hour later, the news of the failure of the Dale-Dustin wild-cat well was flashing far and wide over the wires.

Soon afterward all the world knew of it—that is, all the oil world or the world that cared to know of such things. The greater part of this world rejoiced at the news. It was not exactly envy or jealousy that caused their rejoicing, but perhaps it was a mixture of the two. At any rate it was that unkind feeling that prompts so many of us to secretly dislike the person whom we are congratulating on a success, and, again, to secretly rejoice over his misfortunes, while outwardly sympathizing with him. A few, a very few people were really grieved by the news and were sincerely sorry for the old man and the boy whose hopes were dashed by it.

Deacon Thackby was sorry, but at the same time he found great satisfaction in saying : "You remember I told you how it would be, an I give the Cunnel a fair warnin."

Brace Barlow was sorry; sorry from the very bottom of his great, honest heart; but as he could find no words to express his sorrow he went away without having said that he was.

The scouts were sorry; not that it made any great difference to them, only it would have been so much more fun if the well had proved a "gusher" instead of a "duster." Still, as they philosophically remarked, it would all be the same in the long run. So, after visiting the now lonely and deserted well to assure themselves that the report concerning it was true, they packed their hand-bags and departed in search of new "mysteries." Only one of their number remained behind, and he was the one who, having crouched beside the derrick all night long, was so worn out that he slept through the greater part of the following day. When he awoke his companions had departed, and as the last train of that day had also gone he was forced to remain where he was until the next morning.

To a very small, almost unnoticed portion of the world, the news that the well was a "duster" caused not only unfeigned sorrow, but genuine consternation. Miss Hatty had always been hopeful of its success, while Arthur had never for a moment doubted it. He had such absolute faith that the oil was there and would be found that, with Cynthia's help, he had made plans for years to come, all based upon the striking of oil in the Dale-Dustin well, and the income to be derived from it. He had not only planned the restoration of Dalecourt and laid out his own career as a railroad man, but he had given to all of his friends, and especially to those who had been kind to him and Uncle Phin on their journey, everything that they most desired.

To Cynthia this had all seemed so real that for several days she had been in a state of mental bewilderment, trying to decide upon what she did most desire. To have this responsibility lifted from her mind by the refusal of the oil well to provide even the smallest income with which Arthur's plans might be carried out, was really a great relief to the little girl. Still she could and did sympathize with Arthur's distress, and tried, in her childish way, to comfort him by telling him not to mind, that it did n't matter very much any how, and that there were lots of good times left.

But Arthur did mind, though it was more for his grandfather's sake than for his own. Brace Barlow had awakened him at daylight by throwing pebbles against his window, to tell him the sad news, and ask him to warn his cousins that Colonel Dale had just gone to bed utterly exhausted, and must not be disturbed.

Arthur told Miss Hatty and Cynthia, and, after they had eaten a sorrowful breakfast, they sat and talked of their grief in whispers and low, awed tones, as though somebody had died.

Miss Hatty, who realized more fully than anybody else her uncle's position, and what utter ruin this blow meant for him, was more distressed even than Arthur, and he almost forgot his own sorrow in his efforts to comfort her.

"Don't cry, Cousin Hatty," he pleaded, as he gently smoothed her hair, and wondered in his boyish fashion what good crying could do in such a case as this. "It is n't so bad after all, when you come to think of it," he continued. "Really it is n't. Even if we can't go back to Dalecourt, we have got this place, and it's a great deal better than some places, you know, and your mamma and Uncle Phin can come here to live with us, and I can do lots of things to earn money, and we can be just as happy as anything. I ought to be the one to work for the rest anyhow, because it must have been my knowing so much about oil wells that spoiled this one. I never did feel like a real truly chump, but I thought perhaps you and grandpapa could make up. I am afraid though the trouble was that it was more my well than anybody else's, and so you being chumps did n't do any good."

"You are a dear, blessed little comforter!" cried Miss Hatty, throwing her arms about her "Prince Dusty" and giving him a great hug. She even smiled through her tears, whereupon the boy declared that he could almost see a tiny rainbow at the ends of her eye-lashes.

Then the children went out, but it was only to walk soberly up to the now silent derrick where it was so lonely, and seemed so queer, that they did not care to stay long.

CHAPTER XXXII.

SHOOTING A "DUSTER."

THE long, solemn day wore itself slowly away, and the weight of a great calamity was so heavy upon it that everybody was glad when night came and it was time to go to bed.

Although Colonel Dale had not been seen, he had been heard pacing heavily up and down his room for hours at a time. Miss Hatty had carried some dinner up-stairs, and begged that he would eat it. Without opening his door, he said: "Leave me alone to-day, Harriet, and to-morrow I will again try to face the world." She thereupon left the tray close beside the door, and told him that it was there. He did not again answer her, nor had the tempting dishes been touched at nightfall.

Arthur fell asleep wondering where Brace Barlow had gone, and why his "dear giant" should have left without bidding him good-bye. Perhaps it is for this reason that he sprang from his bed so very wide awake when a tiny pebble rattled against his window, just as it had done the morning before, when Brace roused him to hear the sorrowful news of the well. It was earlier this time than it had been then, for the daylight was so faint that Arthur could just make out that it was his "dear giant" who again stood beneath his window, looking up and beckoning to him.

"Dress yourself and come down as quickly and softly as you can." said the young man, in a loud whisper.

The boy obeyed, wondering what on earth Brace could want with him at that time of day. In less than five minutes he was down stairs, and standing outside, in the damp chill of the early morning.

Brace was waiting for him. Without a word, he led the boy up the hill back of the house, and into the derrick of the Dale-Dustin well. Not until then did he speak. Now he said:

"I have called you out, Arthur, lad, because I have got a job on hand that I can't very well do alone, and because I wanted your permission to undertake it. You own half of this well, don't you?"

"Why, yes," answered the boy, in surprise; "I suppose I do. Grandpapa and I are partners, you know."

"Well, then, as one of the owners, I want your permission to try a shot in it."

"In this well?" cried Arthur; "why, I thought you only shot old wells that had stopped flowing."

"So we do, generally," replied Brace. "But, if a shot will help an old well that won't flow, why shouldn't it help a new one that won't? I've made up my mind that there is oil down in that hole. The sand says there is, and I never knew it to lie. Now, if that is so, it only needs to be stirred up a bit; and a good big shot will fetch it, if anything can. I've been up to the magazine, where I had a little of the stuff left, and have brought down a hundred and twenty quarts. There it is, over yonder."

Arthur gave a little start, as, in the dusky corner of the derrick thus pointed out, he now for the first time saw the well-remembered square tins, in which the terrible explosive rested so quietly.

"I've brought the shells, too," continued Brace. "Now, I only want you to say 'go ahead,' and then help me put into the Dale-Dustin a bigger shot than I have ever used before. It can't do any harm, and it may do a great deal of good. What do you say? Shall we try it?"

"Of course we will!" cried Arthur, greatly excited. "And, oh, Brace! if the oil only would come, shouldn't we be happy?"

"Well, I rather guess we would," replied the torpedo man, heartily, as he began making his preparations for the great shot.

Everything had been made ready, on a liberal scale, for the expected oil that had thus far failed to appear. Two tanks, each capable of holding a thousand barrels, stood empty and waiting. The casing head was in position, and the heavy iron "oil-saver" lay near the well, waiting to be used. Colonel Dale never did anything by halves, and he had been thoroughly prepared for every emergency, except the striking of a dry hole. This he had feared and dreaded, but had not really expected.

In less than an hour, the experienced well-shooter and his fearless young assistant had filled the bright tin tubes with one hundred and twenty quarts of nitro-glycerine, and they now hung in the well, ready to be sent to the bottom as one huge torpedo, eighty feet long. Arthur stood by, without a tremor, as, with steady hands, Brace Barlow emptied can after can of the awful liquid, and was so quick to lend a helping hand whenever he could be of assistance, that he seemed to know what was wanted before the other could utter a request.

So eager and anxious were they, that they hardly spoke while engaged in their dangerous task.

At length the great torpedo was lowered, slowly and carefully, to the very bottom of the well, and its line was reeled in. The empty cans had been carried to a safe distance, and Brace now stood beside the boy, on the derrick floor, holding the go-devil in his hand. He looked at Arthur, and the latter understood the look.

"Yes, Brace," he said, "I want to drop it." With the utmost coolness and steadiness of nerve, 'Prince Dusty' held the iron-winged messenger of destruction over the mouth of the well for an instant, and then sped it on its downward flight, toward the monster waiting a thousand feet below, to receive it.

Hand in hand the man and the boy fled from the place, out from among the trees, and down the hill-side.

Then came a mighty trembling, like that of an earthquake shock, followed by the terrible smothered roar, and a few seconds of silence and suspense.

"There it comes!" shouted Arthur, almost beside himself with excitement, as a liquid column rose slowly from the mouth of the well to a height of twenty feet or so, and then fell back.

"No, that's only the water," answered Brace Barlow, gazing with strained eyes and an intense eagerness, such as he had never before known.

Suddenly a black column of mud, water, and burned glycerine rushed to the top of the derrick. Its blackness was tinged with the yellow of oil, and Brace had opened his mouth to utter a shout of joy; when, with a mighty roar like that of thunder, a dense volume of gas burst forth. For a few moments it enveloped the derrick in an impenetrable, bluish, cloud. As this cleared away there stood revealed a solid golden column, six inches in diameter, reaching to the top of the derrick, and breaking into great jets and fountains of amber-colored spray against the crown pulley.

WITH A MIGHTY ROAR LIKE THAT OF THUNDER, A DENSE VOLUME OF GAS BURST FORTH. (*Page* 264.)

The awful force with which that mighty column of oil rushed upward is beyond conception. Nor can its beauty, as it glowed and throbbed in the red light of the rising sun, be appreciated, save by those who have witnessed similar spectacles.

Miss Hatty, who had sprung from her bed terrified and bewildered by the noise and jar of the shot, saw it as she kneeled by her chamber window, and breathed a fervent prayer of thankfulness.

Colonel Dale, who had rushed into the open air under the impression that some terrible convulsion of nature was at hand, saw it; and, strong man that he was, he trembled like one stricken with a palsy, while great tears streamed down his haggard and deeply furrowed face.

Brace Barlow and Arthur saw it, and the clear morning air rang with their shouts of joy.

"There's no dust in that blessed hole this time!" cried Brace. "She's a 'gusher' if there ever was one, and her like has n't been seen for many a day."

CHAPTER XXXIII.

SAVED BY THE SIGN OF THE TRAMP.

IT rarely happens, in real life, that people are lifted from the profoundest depths of grief, poverty, and misfortune, to such heights of joy and promised prosperity, as was the case with those whose fortunes depended on the success or failure of the Dale-Dustin oil well, on the memorable morning of Brace Barlow's great shot. For many weeks they had been weighed down by anxiety, and filled with mingled hopes and fears. For hours they had been prostrated by what seemed utter and unavoidable ruin. The night had been passed in hopeless sorrow, but in an instant it was swept away. The rising sun, shining full on that gleaming column of oil, hurling its mighty torrent from the mysterious recesses where it had lain hidden for untold ages, filled their hearts with its gladness and unspeakable glory. For some minutes they could only gaze upon the scene that it disclosed with incredulous wonder and amazement.

To Colonel Dale and his niece, who had never before witnessed the shooting of an oil well, the sight was a miracle, and they were at a loss to account for it.

To Arthur and Brace Barlow, who had not dared hope for such wonderful results from their torpedo, that golden fountain of oil was at the moment the most beautiful and desirable thing on earth.

At length, withdrawing his fascinated gaze from it, Arthur saw his grandfather standing bareheaded bewildered, and motionless, near the open door of the frame house. Running to him the excited boy flung himself into his arms, crying:

"Oh, grandpapa, we 've shot the 'duster' and turned it into the most beautiful 'gusher' that ever was seen! Is n't it perfectly splendid! And we are the very most genuine kind of 'chumps,' after all, are n't we? And I never was so happy in all my life! Were you, grandpapa?"

"No, my boy, I don't believe I ever was," answered Colonel Dale, in a voice almost choked with emotion, "unless it was when you came to me to be the joy and pride of my old age."

Then Miss Hatty, who had hastily dressed herself, came running down-stairs; and she cried and laughed at the same time, as she threw her arms about the boy and called him her young "oil Prince," and declared that he was the dearest, and wisest, and most lovable oil Prince in all the world.

Beside them stood shy little Cynthia, gazing at the marvel with wide open eyes, half-frightened and not knowing what to say, but thrilled with the great happiness and excitement of those about her.

In the meantime hundreds of barrels of the precious oil were pouring down the hillside and going to waste, in a yellow stream that fretted and sparkled and tumbled in miniature cascades over the rocks like a runaway mountain brook. Several men from the neighboring farms, attracted by the noise of the explosion and the hoarse roar of the escaping oil and gas, now came hurrying to the spot. Followed by these, Brace Barlow started toward the derrick to see what could be done to check the furious torrent and direct it into the empty tanks.

Colonel Dale was about to join them; but, stopped

by a sudden thought, he turned to Arthur and asked him if he could ride to the telegraph office five miles away and send an important despatch.

"Of course I can, sir," answered the boy promptly, for after his experience of that morning he felt that he could do almost anything.

So a message that had been previously thought out was hastily written. Arthur was charged to make all speed with it and, above all, not to mention a word of what had taken place at the Dale-Dustin well that morning to anybody.

As Colonel Dale had found it necessary to ride about the country a great deal on business connected with the well, he had purchased the horse that Arthur now rode when they first came there. It was a fine animal, and the Colonel valued it highly, besides having grown very fond of it.

Now as, unmindful of Arthur's light weight, it galloped swiftly and easily along the lonely forest roads, it seemed to fully share its young rider's happiness and impatience. Faster and faster they flew, the horse tossing his head and pulling at the bit, while the boy's cheeks became flushed with excitement. His eyes sparkled, and as the fresh morning air whistled passed him it seemed filled with happy fancies. It was a glorious ride, and he was enjoying it to the utmost when it was interrupted in a most disagreeable and unexpected manner.

In the very loneliest part of the road, about half way to the village, two ragged, evil-looking men suddenly sprang out from the bushes by which they had been concealed. One of them succeeded in seizing the bridle of Arthur's horse, and though the startled animal reared and plunged so as to almost unseat his young rider, the man managed to retain his hold. When the horse at last became quiet this man said:

"The walking is good enough for young legs like yours, sonny, so I reckon you'd better light down and lend us this hoss for a bit. My pard here is lame, so that he can't keep up with the procession very well, and we're in a hurry to get along."

"But I am in a hurry too," answered Arthur, trying to speak bravely and to control the fear that had driven every bit of color from his cheeks. "And I am going to the village on very important business."

"It must be *very* important," said the tramp with a disagreeable laugh.

"Yes," spoke up the other, "I reckon it's as important as buying a stick of candy; but that's nothing to the importance of our business. We're walking delegates of the society of independent tramps, we are, and our business can't wait. So tumble down out of that saddle, young feller, without wasting any more of our walyable time. If yer don't I'll pull yer down; for we've got to have this ere hoss."

The word "tramp" was as an inspiration to Arthur, and he answered boldly: "If you steal my horse I shall tell my friend, Sandy Grimes, the very next time I see him, and he will make you send it back, besides making you very sorry that you dared do such a thing."

"What do you know about Sandy Grimes?" asked the man who had the bridle, while they both looked so uneasily at each other that it was evident the name was one they knew and feared.

"He is a friend of mine," replied Arthur, "and he told me I was to mention his name if any tramps like you ever tried to bother me."

"How are you going to prove you are a friend of Sandy's?" asked one of the men. "You don't look over much like one of his kind."

"I'll prove it this way," answered the quick-witted boy. As he spoke, he drew a bit of pencil, and the despatch he was to deliver, from his pocket. On the back of the latter he made the symbol M, that the big tramp, with whose boy he had fought months before, had shown him.

The two tramps look at it in amazement. "Yes, that's Sandy's mark," said one of them at length; "there's no going back on that. But I don't see how he ever come to give it to the likes of you. However, seeing that you've got it, and claims Sandy for a friend, I suppose we've got to let you and the hoss go. You'll have to give us every cent of money that's about your clothes, though, for my pard 'll have to pay his railroad fare, if he can't have a hoss to ride."

Arthur had a dollar that his grandfather had given him, to pay for sending the telegram, and this he willingly gave up. Then, after the men had made him turn all his pockets inside out to show that he had no more money, they let go of his horses'

"YES, THAT'S SANDY'S MARK," SAID ONE OF THEM, "THERE'S NO GOING BACK ON THAT." (*Page 272.*)

bridle, and in another moment he had dashed out of their reach and sight.

It was an ugly adventure, and one that might have ended seriously for him, if the boy had lost his head, or allowed his fright to get the better of him. But, as has been said before, Arthur was not one of the boys who lose their heads in times of danger, and once more his coolness and courage had saved him.

CHAPTER XXXIV.

AN OIL SCOUT OUTWITTED.

ARTHUR reached the telegraph office without further mishap; but, to his dismay, the operator refused to send his message unless it was prepaid,—and he had no money. In spite of Arthur's pleadings that he would do so, and of his offer to go home, get the money, and bring it immediately back with him, the operator steadily refused to send the despatch, saying that it was against the rules to accept a collect message from a stranger.

A young man, who was waiting in the office for a train, and who recognized Arthur as a grandson of the owner of the Dale-Dustin well, listened with interest to this discussion. At length he stepped up to the boy, saying: "I know who you are, and I'll pay for that despatch, rather than have you put to any inconvenience. You can send the money to me at any time by postal note, you know. Let me see how many words there are?"

With this the stranger glanced over Arthur's telegram, as though to count the number of words, at the same time drawing a handful of change from his pocket.

"You must write it out on a regular blank," said the operator; and this the stranger kindly did for Arthur, crumpling up the original when he had finished, and holding it carelessly in his hand, as though there were no further use for it.

Just then the train came along, and the obliging young man hurried away, without giving Arthur his address, or even having told his name.

He was the oil scout, who had hidden beside the Dale-Dustin derrick all night, and thereby learned that the well was a dry hole. When he was comfortably seated in the car, he drew forth the crumpled original of the telegram, and again read it. It was:

"To R. Sims,
    "Petroleum Exchange,
        "Oil City, Pennsylvania:
"Have not struck the oil yet in any quantities. The well now is proving everything bad; but fear a regular duster.
                    "ARTHUR DALE."

"Well, if that is n't one of the clumsiest despatches I ever read," soliloquized the oil scout. "He seems to have tried to work in all the words he could. How absurd to send news like that, twenty-four hours after all the world knew it. I should say that the old Colonel was a little off his base. Perhaps his disappointment has affected his mind. I must drop in on Sims and congratulate him on getting such early information. I'll make him repay me the money I spent on that telegram, too."

Then the scout dismissed the subject from his mind, and turned to the morning paper in which, among other items of oil news, he read of the collapse of the Dale-Dustin mystery, and found himself spoken of in highly complimentary terms as having been the first to discover its true condition.

"That's the ticket," he said to himself, "and it certainly ought to induce a raise of salary. I shall take care that my bosses see that notice, and if they don't come down with something handsome, it won't be my fault or because their duty is not made clear to them."

About three o'clock that afternoon, after having stopped at several other places, the scout reached

Oil City, and sauntered into the office of R. Sims, broker.

"How are you, Sims?" he inquired carelessly, throwing himself into an arm-chair. "What's the latest from Dale-Dustin?"

"Everything is lovely there," answered the broker, who was looking particularly happy and well satisfied at that moment.

"How's that?"

"Why, she's flowing right along, and I got a despatch early this morning that gave me a good three hours' start on the market. It's been a mighty lucky day for Colonel Dale, and not a bad one for yours truly, I can tell you. I should n't be surprised if we 'd netted a cool hundred thousand. By the way, your company got badly left! How did that happen? I thought you were on the spot. The other boys said you were to stay there until to-day."

During these remarks the face of the scout grew white and red by turns. Now he sprang from his chair in a state of the greatest agitation, crying: "What do you mean, man? The Dale-Dustin is a dry hole! What sort of a telegram did you receive this morning?"

"Dry hole! well, I should smile!" exclaimed the broker. "There is the first despatch that I got this morning, and I have had several since confirming it."

With this he handed to the scout a telegraph form on which was written:

"To R. Sims, Petroleum Exchange,
    "Oil City, Pennsylvania:
"Have ~~not~~ struck ~~the~~ oil ~~yet~~ in ~~any~~ quantities. ~~The~~ well ~~now~~ is ~~proving~~ everything ~~bad~~ but ~~fear~~ a ~~regular~~ duster.
                                    "ARTHUR DALE."

"You see," explained Mr. Sims, "we were afraid some of you scouts might bribe the operator, or get hold of our despatches in some way. So we arranged to have all messages referring to the well read just the opposite of what was really meant, until every other word was crossed out. Then you see it comes out all right."

"Oh! it comes out all right, does it?" groaned the scout as he hastily left the office. "Well, it may be for you, but I am afraid it is all wrong for me."

When Arthur returned to the farm after sending his despatch, and with a keen appetite for the breakfast Miss Hatty had saved for him, he found that the great stream of oil had been just got under control, and was rapidly filling the tanks prepared to receive it. He also found a large gang of men at work laying, with all possible speed, a line of pipe from the Dale-Dustin tanks to a pumping station of the great seaboard pipe line that fortunately was located less than a mile away.

The shutting in of that marvellous well was a task that taxed the best energies of Brace Barlow and those who labored with him to their utmost for several hours. When it was finally completed it was a feat to be proud of. Colonel Dale, appreciating the magnitude of the task, offered $400 reward to any one who should succeed in completing it. Stimulated by this, Brace and three other men immediately undertook it.

It was a fearful thing to venture into those floods of falling oil and clouds of suffocating gas; but, in the oil region, men become accustomed to such perils. Stripping to the waist, these four boldly entered the derrick, from the sides of which the boarding had previously been torn away.

There they battled with the rushing torrent, which every now and then flung them and their appliances to one side as though they were jackstraws. Occasionally one, or all of them, would dash out for a few breaths of fresh air, and to rid their lungs of the deadly gases that hung low over the derrick. Then they would return to the fight, and toil with the energy and strength of giants.

At length, under a pressure of nearly three thousand pounds, the oil-saver was slowly forced down upon the fierce stream until its cap finally met the casing head. A moment later the set screws were turned, and the torrent of oil was discharging through four two-inch pipes into the waiting tanks. Its force was as great as though it were impelled by the pump of a steam fire-engine, and the pipes through which it discharged throbbed and vibrated under the terrible pulsations of the flow.

As the men who had accomplished this task came from the derrick, reeking with the oil, they flung themselves to the ground, so thoroughly exhausted with their long struggle that, for nearly an hour, they could not be persuaded to move.

Now the pipe must be hurried to its completion before the tanks overflowed. More men and more teams must be procured. The well could not be closed, or the fierce pressure of the imprisoned oil and gas would blow out its casing, and the waste would be enormous. The tanks were filling at the rate of five hundred barrels an hour in spite of all restrictions that could with safety be placed upon the flow, so that in four hours' time they would be full and running over. So messengers were sent in all directions for more men and teams, until the whole country side was engaged on the work.

Shortly after noon it was finished, and oil from the wonderful Dale-Dustin well was finding its way into the tanks of the great pipe line that would convey it to the distant seaboard refineries.

For months this magnificent well poured out thousands of barrels of oil daily, but after a while it settled down to a steady stream of about five hundred barrels in each twenty-four hours, which yield, with very slight diminution, was continued for several years.

When the wearied, but happy occupants of the little farm-house, retired that night their prospects for the future were as bright and as full of promise as, but a few hours before, they had been sad and gloomy. The well had already more than paid for itself, and it was rapidly yielding them a fortune at the rate of $1,500 for each hour of the day and night. Their days of poverty had come to an end, and wealth was literally flowing in upon them.

It was impossible for Arthur to realize the full meaning of what was happening for his benefit; but his grandfather and cousin did, and their rejoicings were more for his sake than for their own. Even they, however, could have no conception of the effect that the opening of the Dale-Dustin Well was to have upon that whole region, nor of the magical changes that were to take place on that lonely farm within a few days.

CHAPTER XXXV

DEVELOPING AN OIL REGION.

BRACE BARLOW'S great shot not only opened the Dale-Dustin well, but it announced to the world the discovery of a new oil field that promised to be one of the most productive and valuable in the whole Pennsylvania region. As its echoes rolled far and wide over the country, they startled men in all walks of life, bidding them leave their homes and hasten to where the newly-found reservoirs of petroleum only awaited the magic touch of the drill to pour forth their floods of wealth. Thousands of people listened to the call of the echoes, and hundreds gladly responded to them. From all directions they flocked to the Dustin farm. They brought with them wealth seeking opportunities for investment, and they came with empty hands. Experienced oil producers came, and men who had never seen a well or a derrick. Business men, old and young men, came; clerks, store-keepers, hotel men, teamsters, carpenters, well-drillers, and torpedo men, lawyers, doctors, and reporters, men of every age and calling began to pour in to the new oil field the very day after Arthur Dale Dustin dropped the go-devil down its first well.

They came by rail, in wagons, and on foot. They brought their families, and they came without them. Within two weeks the new oil town of Dustindale had sprung into a full-fledged existence. It contained nearly a thousand inhabitants, and its population was increasing by hundreds every day. It was a town of tents, huts, shanties, and the lightest of frame buildings hastily run up at a cost which, in more eligible localities, would have paid for marble structures of the same size. A branch railroad, to connect with the main line, five miles away, was already in process of construction. The lonely Dustin farm was, as though by the touch of a magic wand, transformed into one of the most bustling centres of the busy world.

It was not only a busy place, but a wealthy one; for money poured into it, and was spent as freely as it came. Laborers made ten dollars a day, and teamsters twenty. Thousands of dollars sent to be invested in wells and oil lands changed hands daily. Everybody made money easily and quickly, and the majority of those who did so, seemed possessed of a craze for spending it, giving it away, throwing it away, or doing anything else to get rid of it.

Scores of derricks were to be seen, built or building, in every direction; while by night, as well as by day, was heard the steady clank of walking-beams, and the dull thud of drills.

New wells were going down on all sides; but, for more than a month, only one was in operation. It was the magnificent Dale-Dustin, the magnet that drew this feverish mass of humanity from all places to itself, the living, throbbing promise that kept them there. They gazed at it with a never failing delight and with an ever increasing wonder, as it steadily and without a pause poured forth its thousands of barrels of oil. They began to believe that it was inexhaustible, and that it might flow thus to the end of time. To its owners it was bringing in a royal income. At the same time they had other sources of wealth, more valuable even than it, though but for it these could have had no existence.

Of all this wonderful development and marvellous activity, Colonel Arthur Dale, of Virginia, was King, and his grandson was the Crown Prince.

With the first rush of adventurers to the farm and the first rude growth of Dustindale, little Cynthia was sent to her own home and Miss Hatty returned to Dalecourt. She wanted to take Arthur with her, but he begged so hard to be allowed to stay where he was a while longer that his grandfather consented to let him. So they two lived quietly on in the pleasant old farmhouse, that was destined ere long to stand in the centre of a flourishing town, the marvellous growth of which the boy watched with wondering eyes.

He took a lively interest in every new well being drilled, and went from one to another with wise bits of advice, gleaned from his own experience both as a "chump" and a "sharp." The rig-builders, perched on lofty derricks, loved to look down and see him watching them. Sturdy well drillers smiled as they saw his sober young face, intently studying the motion of the great walking-beams or the turning of the temper screws, and they listened with amused gravity to his decidedly expressed opinions of what should be done or left undone. Profanity ceased as he drew near, and rough words and manners were laid aside until he had passed. He was very proud of being the oldest settler in the town; for, as he said: "You know I lived here long before even you came, grandpapa."

To his grandfather the boy was a never-failing source of pride and joy. He was so gentle and lovable, at the same time so brave and practical and so unspoiled by all the flattery and attention showered upon him, that he was a constant marvel and example to the impulsive old Colonel. To be sure, the latter had never known much about boys; but he certainly had not imagined that, as a class, they were like this one.

For the sake of his grandson, Colonel Dale made the most of the golden opportunities now presented to him. At the very beginning of his operations as an oil producer, he had secured oil leases of large tracts of land lying on both sides of the Dustin farm. For these he was to give one quarter of all the oil produced from them, and guaranteed to sink wells upon them within a certain time. Now he was able to dispose of these leases, in one-acre lots, for a thousand dollars apiece in money, and an agreement that gave him one half the oil.

Within ninety days after the Dale-Dustin well began to flow, half of the Dustin farm had been surveyed into town lots, and sold for half a million of dollars; while the other half was leased in one-acre lots as oil territory, in such a manner as to make it worth as much more. In making these sales, Colonel Dale retained, in Arthur's name, the farmhouse with the land immediately surrounding it, and the Dale-Dustin well.

From all these statements and figures, it will be seen that Arthur's plan for relieving his grandfather's financial difficulties had succeeded beyond his wildest dreams.

As the summer drew near its close, Colonel Dale, impatient to escape from business cares and the intense excitement in which they were living, began to place his affairs in such a shape that he might return to Dalecourt. Arthur, too, was becoming tired of the oil region, and longed for a change of scene. He was therefore made very happy by being told that they would start for Dalecourt early in October, on the very day of the month that he and Uncle Phin had started on their memorable journey a year before. This was also the day set for the formal opening of the branch railroad to Dustindale.

Brace Barlow, who had all this time been in charge of the well that he had opened, was now appointed superintendent of the entire Dale-Dustin interests in that part of the country, at a handsome salary. He was to occupy the farm house, and his mother was to come and live with him.

CHAPTER XXXVI.

ARTHUR REMEMBERS HIS FRIENDS.

ON the evening before they were to go away, Colonel Dale, in his grandson's name, invited all the citizens of Dustindale to assemble on the lawn in front of the farmhouse.

It was a dark night, but the lawn was brilliantly illuminated by hundreds of natural gas torches, that produced a novel and beautiful effect. When the guests arrived—and everybody accepted the invitation—they found that they were to be entertained with fireworks, by the music of the Dustindale Cornet band, by an address from Colonel Dale, and with a supper.

The address was a short one, but it was received with tremendous applause, for it was a presentation, on behalf of Arthur Dale Dustin, to Dustindale, of the plans for a town-hall, a school-house, and a library, accompanied by the money to build and equip them.

Then the people crowded about Arthur, and wanted to shake hands with him, and thank him, and tell him how sorry they were that he was going away, and he tried to answer every one who spoke to him. He could not remember afterwards what he said to anybody, it was all so confusing; but it must have been just what they wanted him to say, for everybody seemed pleased, and somebody said he was such a fine little fellow that he should have been a Prince. Then somebody else took this up, and said he was a Prince, a young oil Prince; which so pleased the fancy of the people that they at once accepted the title, and cheered again and again for their oil Prince.

The next morning, when Arthur walked with his grandfather down to the station of the new railroad, where they were to take the train, he found a crowd of people gathered about and admiring one of the most beautiful private cars that ever was seen. It was attached to the rear end of the passenger train, which was to be the first ever run over that road, and was so new and fresh-looking that it could evidently never have been used. All of its outside metalwork was of gleaming brass, and in a central panel, encircled by a wreath of roses and butterflies, was inscribed, in golden letters, the name "Cynthia."

"Just look at that car, grandpapa!" cried Arthur excitedly. "Is n't it a beauty? and how queer that its name should be Cynthia."

"It is strange," answered Colonel Dale with a smile. "Suppose we step aboard and see what the inside looks like."

They entered by the rear door and found themselves in a beautiful saloon that was furnished with a lounge, table, and easy chairs, and had large plate-glass windows at the end and on both sides. Beyond this was an exquisitely appointed bath-room, and opening from it was a large stateroom, furnished with a low French bedstead, a dressing-table, writing desk, and easy chair. A smaller stateroom opened beyond this one. Still further on they saw a dining-room, at the sides of which were four berths like those in sleeping-cars. Then came a pantry, linen closet, ice chest, and various other conveniences. Last of all was the tiny kitchen, looking like a yacht's galley, and hung all around with the brightest of cooking utensils.

Arthur was charmed with all that he saw and kept wondering who was to ride in this wonderful palace on wheels. As he peeped into the kitchen he hesitated for a moment and then sprang forward with a cry of joy.

There, with a white cap on his head and a snowy apron tied about his waist, was his own dear old Uncle Phin, his face beaming with delighted anticipation.

"Yes, Honey!" he cried, after the tumult of Arthur's greeting had somewhat subsided. "I jes had ter come. Ole Unc Phin couldn' trust you fer ter trabbel wifout him no longer. So I kum to take de charge ob de cookin ob yo kyar."

"My car!" cried Arthur in amazement. "What does he mean by my car, grandpapa?"

"He means," replied Colonel Dale, "that this car, the 'Cynthia,' and all that it contains is, my present to the dearest and best of grandsons, as a slight acknowledgment of what he has done and is doing for me."

"Do you mean that this is my very own car, to travel in, and live in, and do as I please with, grandpapa?" asked the boy, in a slightly awed tone, as the full import of what he had just heard began to dawn upon him.

"Precisely that," was the answer. "And in it, if you choose, we will travel together over all the important railways of the country, while you are taking a course of object lessons in the study of how to become a railroad man. How do you like that for a plan?"

"Why, I never dreamed of one half so splendid!" cried the happy boy. "It is more like a real fairy tale than anything I ever heard of."

Just then a young man, in a handsome blue uniform with shining brass buttons, stepped into the car, and touching his cap to Colonel Dale announced that it was time for the train to start.

Arthur stared at him for a moment and then exclaimed: "Brakeman Joe! Is it Brakeman Joe?"

"Conductor Joe, if you please, sir," said the young man, looking immensely proud and pleased. "Conductor of this car, and at your orders to take her wherever you may choose to have her go."

Then, amid the firing of guns, the cheering of the assembled people, and a great chorus of "good-bye" and "come back again soon," the train moved slowly off, and Arthur had begun his second journey toward Dalecourt. But under what different circumstances from the other was this journey undertaken.

As Arthur sat for a while, perfectly still and thinking it all over, his heart was too full of happiness and gratitude for expression in words. At length he said:

"Grandpapa, I do believe that I am the very happiest boy in the world, and I do wish that all other boys could be as happy as I am."

"I am afraid that all boys do not deserve to be," replied his grandfather, smiling; "though, of course, a great many of them do. At any rate, you now have it in your power to add very greatly to the happiness of all the deserving and unhappy boys whom you may meet. I do not know of any better use to which you can put the great wealth that has been so wonderfully given you; and I am willing you should expend just as much money as you see fit in that way. The very best use we can put money to, is to make others happy with it."

"I think so, too," exclaimed the boy, with flushed cheeks and sparkling eyes; "and I would rather spend all the money you can spare in making people happy, than to do anything else in the world with it. Can't we begin with the people who were good and kind to me, when I was trying to get to you, last year?"

"Of course, we can," answered Colonel Dale. "I had thought of them, and have planned this journey so as to follow as nearly as possible the same route that you and Uncle Phin took, and find all the people we can who were kind to you."

They began to carry out this delightful plan of making people happy that very day, by having the "Cynthia" side-tracked at the station nearest to where the Chapman's lived, and driving to their house.

Nothing could exceed the astonishment of this kind-hearted family at again seeing Arthur, and hearing of all the marvellous things that had happened to him since they last met. Mr. Chapman hitched up his team, and with his wife, and Bert, and Sue, drove over to the railway station, to take dinner with Arthur and his grandfather in the beautiful car.

There they renewed their acquaintance with

Uncle Phin, and made him feel very proud, by praising his cooking, and eating heartily of all the good things that he had provided.

After dinner, Arthur said he wanted to *tell* them a fairy story, instead of reading one to them, as he had done before. It was all about a pretty cottage, near a large city, that had been bought in their name, and was waiting for them. There was also employment waiting for Mr. Chapman in that city, and schools to which Mrs. Chapman could send the children. In the cottage waited the biggest doll that was ever seen for little Sue, while in the cottage stable waited a pony for Bert. The best part of this fairy story was, that it was every word true.

The next stop of the "Cynthia" was in Pittsburgh, where Colonel Dale, and Arthur, and Uncle Phin, all went to see good Aunt Charity, and left the dear old soul staring in tearful amazement at a check for a larger amount of money than she had ever seen in all her life. It was given her for the education of the twins, who were to be brought up to "de whitewash an de kalsomine bizness."

Then they went to Harrisburg, where Conductor Tobin's little house, not far from the railroad, was bought and presented to him, to be his very own for always, and where Kitty Tobin was given the handsomest copy of "Hans Christian Andersen's Fairy Tales" that could be procured.

As they were walking back to the car from Conductor Tobin's house, a boy with a bundle of papers under his arm, stared intently at Arthur for a moment, and then sprang directly in front of him exclaiming:

"Don't yer know me? I'm de kid what you licked one time."

"Why, of course I know you!" cried Arthur, holding out his hand, "and I am very glad to see you. How do you do, Kid?"

Then the Kid said his name was Billy Grimes, and that ever since he heard Arthur read that story he had been trying to be something better than an ugly duck. He had run away from his father in Pittsburgh, soon after meeting Arthur, because the big tramp wanted to make him steal for a living, and had gradually worked his way to Harrisburg, where he was trying to be an honest newsboy.

The result of this fortunate second meeting with Arthur was that, in less than a month from that time, Master William Grimes was entered as a pupil in one of the best military schools of the country. There he is working so hard and doing so well that, before long nobody will remember that he ever was an "ugly duckling."

In Washington Colonel Dale went to call on an old friend, and took Arthur with him. To the boy's surprise and delight, this friend proved to be the very gentleman to whom he had sold his dog Rusty. The dog was still there, and manifested such extravagant joy at again seeing his former master that the gentleman laughingly said it would be cruel to part such loving friends any longer. So the dear dog, now more handsome and knowing than ever, was again presented to the boy who had once fought to save him from a beating, and Arthur said this was the happiest thing of the whole journey.

The next day they were once more at Dalecourt, and the very first person Arthur saw, standing in the doorway as he and Rusty sprang from the carriage, was Cynthia. Colonel Dale had invited her to come to Dalecourt to be educated and to live as his daughter, and her father had consented that she should.

Miss Hatty had been engaged all summer in restoring Dalecourt to even more than its former glory, so that now it was one of the most beautiful places in Virginia.

Here we must leave the boy whose wanderings and fortunes we have followed for a year. Although he is no longer poor, he studies and works just as hard as though he were, and is all the happier for so doing. He is still determined to be a railroad man when he grows up, and he still finds his chief pleasure in turning other people's sorrow into happiness.

On that first evening at Dalecourt Miss Hatty went up to his room to take away the light after he had gone to bed. He was just dropping to sleep as she bent over him, and kissing his forehead said softly: "Good-night and pleasant dreams to you, my dear little Prince Dusty!"

THE END.